RECOVERING A

CATHOLIC PHILOSOPHY OF

ELEMENTARY EDUCATION

RECOVERING A CATHOLIC PHILOSOPHY OF ELEMENTARY EDUCATION

Curtis L. Hancock

with a Foreword by Peter Redpath

NEWMAN HOUSE PRESS

RECOVERING A CATHOLIC PHILOSOPHY OF ELEMENTARY EDUCATION
ISBN 0–9704022–8–7

Copyright © 2005 Newman House Press
21 Fairview Avenue, Mount Pocono, PA 18344

PRINTED IN THE UNITED STATES OF AMERICA

Contents

Foreword

Western civilization faces a crisis of philosophical identity. As the author of this book well understands, solving this crisis partly involves recovering a proper understanding of Catholic education, including the proper function of Catholic elementary schools.

Catholicism connects Western civilization's philosophical identity with its historical roots. Ignorance of the Catholic educational tradition prevents us from recovering a proper understanding of our philosophical past, especially its metaphysical, moral, and political dimensions. Contemporary Western civilization has intimate Christian metaphysical, moral, and theological roots—in the Church's teaching about creation and the dignity of the human person flowing from the Incarnation, and in the classical Greek and Roman philosophical traditions. From these intellectual roots developed modern science and democratic government, and this process continues. Without them, Western civilization cannot survive.

No civilization can long endure once it loses faith in its founding metaphysical and moral principles. No political body can long survive once it loses sight of what it is, where it came from, how it got where it is, and where it is going; these are its metaphysical and moral principles. In the West, we get these principles chiefly from our theological and classical philosophical heritage.

Metaphysical and moral principles are the first (and ultimate) measures of human knowledge and human choice. We cannot possibly divorce education, art, science, politics and civilization from our thinking about human nature, the people, things, and faculties that activate human actions are first principles of human actions, philosophy and education included.

Education is the art of using our knowledge of the nature of things around us and of ourselves: liberating ourselves from the slavery of ignorance, bad choice, and disordered delight and thus improving our lives. Mortimer J. Adler has correctly said that human education is an art of using knowledge about ourselves and things around us "to prevent and cure ignorance, to sustain and improve what one might call mental or spiritual health."[1] Human education is the art of using knowledge about ourselves and things around us to develop excellent human habits (virtues) of judging, choosing, reasoning, and enjoyment.

In still other words, human education is an art whereby we become increasingly virtuous, improving ourselves in our ability to acquire, develop, and mature in human knowledge and in our use of human freedom. Education, then, has two natural human ends: developing the virtues of wisdom and fostering the habits of prudence. Catholic education exists for the further, more-than-natural, end of getting us to Heaven. Human nature itself and the natures of things around us, not musings about human self-definition, set these goals. Ignorance produces a slavery from which our human nature drives us to escape by inclining us to improve the quality of our minds and the way we live our lives—to become virtuous.

Such goals play a part in our reflection upon the condition of contemporary Western education. Our proper understanding of education faces three blockades to evaluating or reforming our own education: (1) vested educational interests, (2) inertia in the teaching profession, and (3) the inbred relationship between education and politics.[2]

Regarding the first obstacle, Adler says in a colorful metaphor: "*Organized education is one of the largest rackets in this country, and the teachers colleges, especially such influential ones as those at Columbia, Chicago, and California, are the gangs that control what goes on, in ways that do not always meet the eye and would not stand inspection.*"[3]

Regarding the second and third obstacles, Adler notes that "a vicious circle exists in the teaching profession" and always tends to exist when human institutions become standardized. In this instance, "a philosophy of education becomes an official program imposed upon the profession and the system by various accrediting agencies, degrees, requirements for promotion, and so forth." When this happens, "the circle becomes almost impregnable. Even if the great mass of teachers were to feel that there is something wrong with education, they could do nothing about it. They have been subjugated; worse than that, they

[1] Mortimer J. Adler, "Are There Absolute and Universal Principles?" in *Reforming Education: The Opening of the American Mind* (New York: Macmillan Publishing Company, 1988), p. 56.

[2] Ibid., pp. 78–79.

[3] Ibid., p. 78. The emphasis is Adler's.

have been indoctrinated by the reigning philosophy so that they no longer have enough free judgment to be critical; but worst of all, they themselves have been so inadequately educated that they would be hindered from understanding the principles or taking part in the execution of the reform being proposed."[4]

The net result of any such indoctrination is over-training and under-education. Most of our school teachers today are over-trained and under-educated.

The teaching art presupposes an intellectually and linguistically cultivated mind. The teacher's art is that of communicating learning arts about ourselves and the things around us, arts of listening and speaking, reading, writing, measuring, judging, choosing, reasoning, and qualitative discernment about the truth, goodness, and beauty—of things and of ourselves.

Under an institutionalized education, as Plato recognized centuries ago, a culture tends to develop in a circle, Adler's third "vicious, circle."[5] The institutionalized educational principles and the social habits they produce tend to influence each other reciprocally. To improve a society, we have to better its educational institutions. To better its educational institutions, we have to better the society. How do we avoid the vicious circle when we have been indoctrinated in false educational "philosophy" that we need to transcend to get out of the circle?

We do so by our natural ability to reason about the things around us and about ourselves. Eventually we recognize that, strictly speaking, this "philosophy" is no philosophy at all. Philosophy, like physical science, starts in wonder: with limited knowledge about things around us and ourselves, not with error or doubt. To get out of a racket and to avoid the vicious circle it produces, we have to recognize that we belong to a racket in the first place. This is as true of philosophers as it is of anyone else.

Next, we have to clear our minds of the false views of ourselves and our world with which we have been indoctrinated. In the late 1930s, Adler thought that these views were philosophies of materialism, pragmatism, and modernism. While Adler was right that, to reform contemporary education, including Catholic education, we have to rid ourselves of such mistaken views, but he was wrong to call them

[4] Ibid., pp. 78–79.
[5] Adler, "Are There Absolute and Universal Principles?" p. 79, and Plato, *Republic* 424A–426E.

"philosophies." They are today's sophistries, systems of falsehoods, and ignorance, about ourselves and the world that can be traced—in the West at least—as far back as René Descartes.

As Catholics, we soon escape these false views by recalling our metaphysical and theological heritage, by recalling who we are, how we got here, where we are going, and why we are going there. We are human beings, finite created beings, composed of a corruptible body and an immortal soul, made by an almighty Trinitarian Creator God, in His image and likeness. We got here through God's free gift of creation. We are working our way toward Heaven. And we get to Heaven through the grace of faith and participation in the Church's sacramental life and through the gifts of the Holy Spirit.

Materialism and modernism are false because they take no account of spiritual realities or even the reality of mystery. Pragmatism is wrong because not all human truth, not every human good, is practical. Some human truths are more and greater than practical, more and greater than useful. For example, the delightful truth that a person we love is alive, or the contemplation of the truth that only God can create the universe *ex nihilo*.

After we jettison our materialism, pragmatism, and modernism, we set aside all current sophistry and recognize that, simply put, we have no philosophy of education and, indeed, no philosophy at all. We have to develop them.

To develop a philosophy of education as Catholics, we see that Catholic faith must illumine such a philosophy. We must build it upon a Catholic understanding of the human person, the supernatural ends of the human person, and the means to achieve these ends—because the goal of all human education is to help us make ourselves all that we can be, to bring ourselves to perfection in the exercise of the human operations we produce through habitual exercise of our *educating* faculties, that is, our highest human faculties. We find the *ends* of human education in the things around us and the way they are related to human nature and its goals.[6]

We educate ourselves chiefly through our intellects, because we educate ourselves by increasing our knowledge, that is, we increase our knowledge chiefly through our intellects. Other of our faculties do

---

[6] Adler, "Are There Absolute and Universal Principles?" p. 57.

participate in our education, but they do so by *cooperating* with the human intellect in the work of personal education.

Educational faculties are a personal coincidence of intellectual and other human faculties. Examples of such other powers are our five external senses, our internal senses of imagination and sense memory, and our emotions and will. To some degree, we may call each of these faculties "educational" or "intellectual" because, in some way, they involve a cooperative activity of human intelligence and other determinate human powers.

Some people settle on the notion that we develop our intellectual ability after we acquire a lot of sense knowledge. In truth, we "sense" nothing without intellectual awareness; and, in this life, we have no intellectual awareness without simultaneously sensing something. Human intelligence in this life is not purely intellectual or sensory. It is a coincidence of both; it is *personal*. Our intellect is present in the first act of sensation, and our senses are present in our first act of intelligence. The mark of intelligence, therefore, is *judgment*, not sensing, imagining, or abstract conceptualizing.

We often speak of making "uneducated" choices, choices devoid of right intellectual direction. When making choices, however, the only thing we can directly *choose* is some human *action*. We do not directly choose external things, which are but instruments that make possible our performance of human actions. For example, we do not directly choose a knife or a fork. We choose (humanly) "to hold" a knife or a fork, to engage in the act of eating. We directly choose *to hold* and *to eat*, not the knife or the fork. We do not directly choose socks or shoes. We directly choose "to wear" socks or shoes.

These are major, not minor, points about human activity. Human activity is living, personal. When we indirectly choose something that helps us carry on such activity, we do so by enabling this thing to participate (instrumentally) in living, personal action. We give it intellectual direction and form through participation in intellectually directed human powers, such powers as our external body parts and the senses that activate these parts. And we give our intellects bodily direction by limiting them to participation in sensory activity. *Wearing* (clothes) and *holding* (tools) are sense *and* intellectual activities. The way a person wears clothes or holds a knife and fork is personal, intellectual, and physical. So also are all human actions, riding, swimming, walking, dancing, reading, and so forth.

Because human education is personal and involves cooperation between the human intellect and human faculties that (in some degree) can co-direct each other, to have a complete understanding of human education, as the author of this book notes, we have to have some understanding of the faculties that the human intellect can influence and that can influence the human intellect—and of how all this occurs.

These faculties may be listed in five groups: (1) external (the five external senses), (2) internal (general sense, imagination, emotions, sense memory, i.e., memory of concrete sense details, and particular reason), (3) intellectual memory (memory of abstract generalizations), (4) will, and (5) intellect.

We *become* educated by getting our educational faculties to work together or cooperate to increase our knowledge. By this process, we become (so to speak) more human than we were; we grow intellectually and develop as persons. The whole task of education involves getting our faculties to work together, to cooperate, to grasp or produce the human good. As Catholics, we easily understand that this action involves overcoming the effects of original sin.

We become "most human" when we excel at performing personal actions through the cooperation between the (a) excellent exercise of our highest powers of intelligence and choice and (b) our lower sensory powers. "Virtuous" is a name we often use to refer to excellent human beings, those who excel other human beings at living a moral life or in what we call "being human." We often use the word "skillful" to refer to human beings who excel other human beings in their ability to get their human faculties to cooperate, harmonize, coincide, or work together, to do or make things exceptionally good for improving human life. Virtuous or skillful people, in short, have exceptional ability to get their human faculties of intellect, sense, will, and emotion to work together to do humanly exceptional things or exceptionally human things.

Human education is human nature's call to human virtue, because by human virtue we become all that we each can be. Human virtues are our educational "methods," the means to human happiness. And human education is inculcation in human happiness. By nature, in brief, we incline to pursue knowledge and avoid ignorance because (as Aristotle understood centuries ago) without knowledge we cannot become happy in this life or the next.[7]

---

[7] Aristotle, *Metaphysics*, Bk. 1, Ch. 1, 982a1–981b35.

Knowledge is not enough to become happy in this life or the next, but it is a necessary precondition. Similarly, knowledge is not enough for education. Human education involves more than knowledge; it calls for human goodness, making our faculties and actions good, getting them to cooperate to recognize and do humanly good things.

To become educated, we make our human faculties good and use them well. In its precise sense, human education is the education of human faculties in their own good exercise, in human goodness—virtue. By nature, the overall end (objective) of all human education is to produce a good human being, a being who acts humanly well, who lives well or excellently. It follows that dire consequences must befall any purported philosophy of education that bases itself on a flawed understanding of human nature. No such philosophy of education can be a philosophy at all, nor can it educate.

Catholic education sees perfection of the human person as education's natural and supernatural end; this means, first, that Catholic education's main aim is to produce good Catholics, to produce good Catholic human beings, human beings who love God and neighbor as themselves and thus get to Heaven. These are Christ-like individuals (or saints). If Catholic philosophy of education forgets this aim, it is no "philosophy" at all.

The primary *means* of Catholic education lie in training or disciplining the human faculties in all the human virtues so that they cooperate to do humanly good things. It follows that Catholic teachers begin with an understanding of what human faculties they can educationally train and how they go about the process. The faculties they educationally train are those that can take direction from right reason, that is, reason directed by knowledge. Human freedom does not lie in the *absence* of a rule directing our human actions; it involves "submission to a right rule."[8] Education liberates our faculties by intellectually qualifying them to participate in the rule of right reason. Wisdom and prudence free us from slavery because these two intellectual virtues qualify our emotions and appetites, thereby enabling us to master our human faculties and to apply them rightly to the individual situation, so as to discern truth and to enjoy the exercise of excellent choice.

[8] Mortimer J. Adler, "Liberalism and Liberal Education (1939)," in *Reforming Education: The Opening of the American Mind*, p. 51.

Catholic education is a liberation movement that gives us mastery of all our learning faculties by qualifying them through direction by right reason.

As human beings, we are born with different external and internal sensory, emotive, and appetitive faculties that are immaturely developed, and we incline by nature to cooperate with, to take direction from, rightly guided human reason so that we might bring ourselves, as persons, to mature and healthy development. People who know about such things and can pass their knowledge on to others through intellectually elevating conversation should be our teachers, because they are the ones who *can* communicate it. As Adler has nicely said, education is elevation of our intellects by our intellectual betters.[9] The method of Catholic education is always conversational, speaking and listening and their various modes, conversing with the intellectual superiors around us about the natures of things and people. In short, in its most precise sense, the teacher's art is liberal, drawing upon a cultural heritage of great intellectual discovery rooted in accurate knowledge about ourselves and the things around us—the "liberal arts education" that stands on the shoulders of giants. As such, the teacher's art presupposes a cultural heritage and conversation with cultivated minds, a tradition of virtue-laden conversation, not rote-method classes or study based on flawed human psychology, mistaken pedagogy, or simplistic intellectual content.

This must be the nature of the teacher's art because teaching is a cooperative art, much like farming. It presupposes fertile soil and proper cultivation of that soil, mentally and physically qualified minds and bodies.

Mentally qualified student minds are those receptive to learning and taking direction from their intellectual betters. Students who lack the proper emotional and volitional mindset to take directions cannot learn. Neither can students who are distracted by severe physical ailments or other impediments to teachability, including excessive distractions of one sort or another.

Mentally qualified teaching minds are those inclined to sharing their knowledge by conversing and cooperating with their intellectual inferiors. Intelligent people who lack the right emotional and volitional mindset cannot teach. Neither can people who are impeded by exces-

[9] Mortimer J. Adler, *How to Read a Book* (London: Jarrolds Publishers, Ltd., 1949), pp. 33–35.

sively severe physical ailments or other impediments to sharing their learning because of one sort of distraction or another.

However, teaching requires something more: it requires the superior knowledge that an artistic and scientific mind possesses. Properly speaking, teaching involves guiding other persons to come to *know* by leading them to imitate the sort of reasoning process the teacher uses to discover and communicate a truth.

Teaching occurs through intellectual imitation. The person who knows something best is the person who knows with greatest precision the closest, most intimate, and most minute causes for a thing's existence and operations. Because such a person knows best what causes things to exist and operate the way they do ("first principles"), this person deserves the name "teacher." And this person should be best at explaining to others why something is the way it is and behaves the way it does. The architect-teacher tends to be better than others at teaching us the principles and causes that enable buildings to withstand stress and support a specific structure's configuration and weight.

Teaching involves directing a person's intellect by causing that intellect to share in rightly directed reasoning through explanations guided by a knowledge of causes. Teaching is thus in essence an intellectually elevating conversation.

Because teaching is intellectually elevating conversation and a cooperative art, we rightly apply the term "teacher" (with unequal precision) to many subjects of unequal ability. In a strict application of the word, only the artist or scientist deserves the name because only the artist or scientist, the best of discoverers, can explain to others with utmost precision the most proximate and minute causes for different occurrences, explaining something in terms of its first, most universal, and highest cause. Such is the way, for instance, that we apply the word to master builders and architects. In a wider sense, we may apply the name "teacher" to anyone with more causal knowledge than another person who can use that knowledge to give someone an improved understanding of the reason why something happens. In this sense, a carpenter on a job site can "teach" a prospective home-buyer why a particular material is being used rather than another by a simple explanation ("Because the architect said to use this material" or "We had good experience with this material").

Such analogous use of the term "teacher" is crucial to understanding that more than one kind of teacher, and more than one kind of student, is involved in human, and Catholic, education. On every level (higher, middle, or lower), human and Catholic education has many teachers and learners. On whatever level, the chief teacher is the person who (1) knows something best and (2) is best able to communicate this knowledge to others. In most instances, this main teacher is not the classroom teacher. Not to recognize this fact is a grave mistake.

The better teachers are the more knowledgeable and the better communicators. Sometimes, however, even the most knowledgeable person might not be the best communicator—might be sick or severely disabled, or, because of weak language skills, might not be able to say well what he knows. Hence, in the practical order, human education requires a multitude of teachers.

Often, some children are better than adults at communicating adult matters to other children because the children readily understand how to put these things into language children readily understand and adults have forgotten. We teach the way we can, not the way we wish. Being able to teach involves being able to put things into a language another person can understand. And, at times, this is not something a great discoverer knows how to do. Hence, aside from great discoverers, human education needs secondary teachers, people who help beginning students participate in the intellectual discoveries of great intellects by translating these discoveries into language that beginning students can understand.

Naturally, elementary (lower) education begins in the home with conversations between parents and children, with home schooling. All further education is an analogous transposition of this primary education, of talking to and reading with our children. In a way, then, all education is home schooling or an analogous transposition of home schooling. Higher education terminates in the cultural order with great conversations between highly educated students and great discoverers.

Most education lies between these two extremes. Highest education terminates for a Catholic in the beatific conversation between Christlike, saintly people and the Persons of the Trinity.

We get from the lowest level to the highest through the exercise of intellectual and moral virtues. Hence, elementary education is education in elementary intellectual and moral virtues, training a child's lower educational faculties to become receptive to learning and taking direction by reason.

Before the "age of reason," that is, before the child has reached the level of moral self-awareness and control, children still have the ability, more or less, to listen to reason. The main aim of all elementary education, and of higher education too, is to get people to listen to rightly guided reason.

Formal elementary education is an adult-assisted training of a child's senses and emotions, a participation of a child's senses under the direction of adult intelligence. Children are naturally inclined to listen to adult reason in the same fashion that our sense faculties are naturally inclined to take direction from our sense of sight or adults and children are naturally inclined to accept intellectual direction from people we think know more than we do. We all tend to act this way because we are naturally inclined to follow direction by rightly guided reason more than we are inclined to follow any of our other human faculties or sort of reason.

In most everyday situations, this elementary education takes place with several children. Its natural mode should be friendly conversation. It starts with a child's understanding of the things around the child and of the child's sensory self. We begin teaching children by linguistically familiarizing them with themselves through sensory contact with the things around them and themselves. We start to teach them by talking with them in a language they can understand, using intellectual conversation between adult and child so that we can first learn what they already know. We do this to try to get their sense faculties to cooperate with our linguistic direction.

When we do this in a group setting, we have to get all the children involved as cooperative, secondary teachers and learners. Hence we start this process by trying to develop group conversation among friends. We get the students to talk to one another so as to know one another better.

One of the first steps of any teacher is to begin by befriending students and wishing them well, being willing to listen to them, sharing our learning with them, and helping them to befriend one another. One of the things a classroom teacher must do, then, is to create a "learning atmosphere" of friendship, in which students are inclined to cooperate with one another and their teacher in intellectual conversation. Then too a classroom teacher's second goal is to recognize that classroom teaching involves coordinating the activity of a multitude of teachers and learners.

Learning is a lifelong cooperative venture involving a multitude of teachers and students of varying abilities. The more we can harness the cooperation of this multitude to elevate our intellects, the taller and wider become the shoulders of the intellectual giants upon which we stand, to become all that we can be.

A third goal of any teacher is to get students to reflect repeatedly on who they are, why they are where they are intellectually and emotionally, where they came from, and where they are going. A fourth is to form students into a reading circle or circle of learning. Learning is a cooperative human activity that we achieve mainly through conversation. Hence the classroom teacher properly works to engage students in cooperative reading of, and conversation about, books of exceptional quality. We are more likely to increase our intelligence by constantly conversing with intelligent people than we are by talking with mediocre or dull intellects. This is true on every level of education. We do not have to be geniuses to recognize this simple truth: The main teacher in most educational settings is the good book.

Elementary education is primarily "elementary" training of the external senses, bringing the external senses under rational direction, centered on conversations about a good book. Human beings use their memory and imagination to direct their senses and emotions. This natural process explains why we can so easily alter people's emotional states by causing them to recall imaginary situations. Memory and imagination are essential instruments used in elementary (and all) education. In elementary education, we focus attention on educating the sense memory in cooperation with the imagination to develop a child's sensory motor skills as we direct these, in cooperation with good books, toward mastering abilities in listening and speaking, reading, writing, measuring, and enjoying abilities.

Elementary education involves imbedding our sense faculties with the linguistic directions we get from great teachers through good books, habituating these faculties to follow good linguistic directions: getting the growing external and internal senses to do what better minds reasonably tell them. For this reason (among others), all human education involves training in the liberal arts. And, because this process involves direction by memory and imagination, the ancient Greeks first called human education "music," education by the Muses, the goddesses who influence memory and imagination to assist in developing liberal learning.

In a Catholic setting, this education involves several other teachers: the internal teacher, Christ, who guides us through the direction of the Holy Spirit in the Church's sacramental life; the Magisterium; and parents.

Just as we constantly remind children about the physical things around them and themselves as physical, emotional, and intellectual beings and children, as Catholics we should constantly remind them about the spiritual realities that surround them, their spiritual nature, and their status as children of God. Catholics do this through sacraments and spiritually significant and symbolic life.

We physically communicate knowledge about intellectual, emotional, and spiritual realities through the use of physical beings, signs and symbols. As physical beings, we are totally incapable of conveying our thoughts and emotions to other people without the use of linguistic signs and symbols. Signs and symbols play a crucial role in all education, especially in the spiritual life.

We educate children and ourselves in virtue through signs and symbols. We do this through physical and psychological acts of speaking and listening, reading and writing, measuring, painting, sculpting, singing and dancing. Deprived of participation in a richly significant and symbolic life, we human beings die intellectually, emotionally, culturally, and spiritually. Hence, no Catholic education worthy of the name can expect to succeed without rich participation in the Church's sacramental life and respect for the Magisterium.

Finally, all elementary education is primarily an extension of parental education; it is extended and cooperative home schooling. Authentic elementary schools are cooperative and extended home schools. Rich family life is human education's best elementary setting. Parents, not elementary schools, the State, or the Church, have the main moral responsibility of educating children to adulthood. While no parent knows all the things a child should learn, neither does every classroom teacher, administrator, cleric, or politician. And while schools are extensions of the home, homes are not, and never should be, extensions of the school.

Elementary education starts and remains in the home, and elementary school teachers and administrators reinforce and assist this effort in home schooling. To distort this relationship of school to home is to disorder elementary education and to undermine its essential nature as familial conversation.

Because elementary education is chiefly familial conversation with great teachers, absence of parental involvement necessarily weakens elementary school education.

Because parents have a moral responsibility to educate their children to adulthood, they have a moral responsibility to find their children good teachers when they cannot teach their children themselves. For both parents and elementary schools, these good teachers are mainly authors of great books, *the* great discoverers. For Catholics, they are, among others, the great Catholic intellects and spiritual writers. To put children in touch with them is the great mission of Catholic education.

Peter A. Redpath
St. John's University
Staten Island, New York

Preface

Some years ago, the university where I teach in the department of philosophy asked me to advise students matriculating through the curriculum toward certification as elementary and secondary teachers. An "outside" person was needed, and during the two years of my service, I enjoyed many conversations with bright, eager students, and with their often accomplished professors. However, as a trained philosopher, I could not help but notice that sometimes these same students and professors made philosophical remarks, even if they did not recognize them as such. Their observations commonly took the form of "orthodoxies" or "dogmas," remarks said and heard so often that they were regarded as obvious, as platitudes. Occasionally, these remarks were judgments about philosophy itself. A look of bemusement was the typical response, were I politely to challenge any of these beliefs.

These dogmas were much on display at a meeting I attended along with other faculty, including those from the Department of Education. Curriculum matters in general and requirements for teacher certification were under discussion. During that meeting, I said little. Instead, I jotted down remarks that were philosophical or in need of philosophical examination. I recorded such remarks (some of them in paraphrase) and tucked them away for a later time, in the hope that I would have an opportunity someday to discuss with my colleagues how philosophy is implicit whenever educators reflect on the nature of their work. I list here a sampling of a host of such observations expressed that afternoon. (I will limit my list to eleven; I don't like to list ten of anything.)

"As people become less religious, they become civilized."

"Philosophy is too vague, general, and impressionistic a subject to address satisfactorily the specific issues needed for directing educators today."

"Modern science has been able to answer most of the problems of philosophy."

"The ancient problems science cannot now answer, it surely will someday."

"Philosophy has been replaced by social science."

"Learning is brain activity. The future of education lies in knowing how the brain works."

"Nobody can ever really judge what is right or wrong."

"The goal of education is for each child to find his or her own truth."

"The goal of education is for each child to invent his or her own values."

"Instruction in sex and sexuality has become far too complex and technical to leave to the typical parent."

"Good schools are the last hope for making society better."

Clearly, this sampling of "bold assertions" calls out for philosophical examination. Each statement is controversial, assuming we even know what it means, which is itself an important element in any philosophical examination: clarifying terms. I have highlighted these eleven statements because, if we naïvely accept them, they convey claims that, in my judgment, make genuine Catholic education impossible. Moreover, these remarks show how readily and commonly we encounter philosophical assertions about education in the academic milieu.

I never had a chance to discuss these remarks with my colleagues during or after the aforementioned meeting. This book provides my chance. I may take up directly only a few of the eleven propositions in this and subsequent chapters, but I will address them all to some degree. By absorbing the philosophical principles and arguments of this book, readers should learn how to assess such assertions about teaching and learning. And, in making that assessment, the reader will know how to vindicate a Catholic philosophy of elementary education.

C. L. H.

CHAPTER ONE

Why a 'Catholic' Philosophy of Elementary Education?

To begin, some words on philosophy are in order. Many people today, some of them credentialed with graduate degrees, have little exposure to the discipline of philosophy. Some of this unfamiliarity is a result of what has happened to the discipline of philosophy over the past few centuries. Philosophy as it is taught in academic institutions today has become very narrow and "professionalized," so much so that it holds out little interest for educated people outside the university bureaucracy. Often it is available only as electives in college curricula. As a result, many students, even those seeking a liberal education, are unsure about whether they should include philosophy among their courses of study. Moreover, their college advisors are often likewise unsure. At many colleges and universities, philosophy was long ago eliminated from the list of required courses. Many administrators and faculty regard philosophy as a curiosity, a holdover from bygone curricula, a vestige of an outdated humanistic education preserved to placate nostalgics.

Even those who escape this prejudgment and who actually enroll in a philosophy course often find the experience unsatisfying, dismissing the subject as obscure and gratuitously difficult. They frequently leave the course doubtful of philosophy's relevance to society, skeptical of its value for a highly literate and educated public. That was an attitude expressed by my colleagues at the meeting I alluded to earlier. They often resisted the suggestion that they were themselves making philosophical statements because (*a*) they had "taken philosophy" in college and were sure what they were saying had no connection with that unpleasant experience; and (*b*) philosophy for them is a pre-scientific way of looking at education, and they took pride in being involved in the cutting-edge, *scientific* advances of education.

This attitude is no surprise. Outside of specialists within departments of philosophy in universities, few people occupy themselves with what philosophers say, and fewer still venture to articulate contemporary philosophical theories and fashions. What philosophers say and teach is increasingly ignored. Because philosophers are largely ignored today, a tendency exists to think that their cultural influence is negligible. True enough, few philosophers today are widely known; hardly any are recognizable names and faces in the public square. But ideas do have consequences, and the work of past and present philosophers continues to exercise a powerful influence on modern culture, for good and for ill. But most of their influence passes into and through other disciplines and other voices of culture, who express and work out, often ignorant of their influence, the results of the work of philosophers.

The influence of philosophers in society is real and powerful, even if their influence is sometimes "below the radar." Their influence is something every educated person should notice. If we expect to participate in informed discourse, we cannot afford to be ignorant of philosophical ideas and their percolation in culture, Because philosophical ideas have cultural consequences, a person who is ignorant of how these ideas have shaped and continue to shape cultural trends will be moved to the sidelines during the march of social change. If such persons have issues they would like to champion, and if they are not conversant with the philosophical ideas behind the vocabulary and the fashions of those who use their philosophical skills to monopolize the marketplace of ideas, they will be sitting ducks before those who covet such cultural power. History is a record of those who were derelict in the wake of change affected by this or that philosophical idea in this or that culture war.

Though one's experience with philosophy may be doubtful, unproductive, or unpleasant, knowledge of philosophy is necessary if one is to understand cultural change. Such understanding is more than an academic matter. Philosophy's academic value is secondary to its power to make us culturally aware. Philosophy's presence in our lives carries profound *personal* and *practical* value.

Sadly, what passes as "academic" philosophy often causes us to forget the true value of philosophy. Even though philosophy as promulgated out of universities is often ignored, it continues to influence the culture. The neglect "professional" philosophy suffers in the public square, however, is tragic only if philosophers still have something constructive to say. Alas, much evidence suggests they do not. Philosophy has become so narrow because of modernist skepticism and relativism that it has little to contribute to people who want something that resembles what a person classically trained in earlier times would have called "wisdom."

This current situation evokes the question, "If philosophy is in a sickly state, where do we go to find a salutary philosophy?" The answer lies in finding an alternative philosophy, one that escapes the professional deformations of academic philosophy. This alternative philosophy would be attractive to educators because they would readily intuit its relevance. It would not be met with the indifference or revulsion that often greets the subject in many (but not all) departments of philosophy at universities.

The ancient Greeks identified and cultivated an authentic way of philosophical knowing. This philosophy is the source of a wisdom that can still inform and edify today's educator. Here, then, is my effort to recover this ancient wisdom, explain its influence in the formation of Catholic thought and teaching, and demonstrate the relevance of this philosophy to the contemporary elementary teacher in a Catholic school. When I speak of philosophy, I refer primarily to the discipline as it was first understood by the Greeks and later assimilated into the wisdom of the Catholic Church.

Let me begin by considering what philosophy meant to the ancient Greeks and then take up the way the Catholic Church absorbed the spirit of Greek philosophy while transforming it into "Christian philosophy," a philosophy in concert with Christian theological wisdom.

Words change. Their change may preserve their original meaning, or their alteration may be more of a mutation, out of which they come to mean something significantly different. What *philosophy* means today bears little resemblance to what it meant to the ancient Greeks, who originally discovered and explained the subject as a distinct way of knowing. "Philosophy" today tends to mean logic. This is a far cry from Aristotle's warning that logic is not philosophy; it is not even a branch of philosophy. Logic is a skill that a philosopher must have, but it is not, properly speaking, a part of philosophy. It is, Aristotle insists, a *tool* for philosophers, but not philosophy itself.

For the ancient Greeks, philosophy was a response, inspired by wonder, to life's perplexities. As such, philosophy had its natural starting place in experience, not in words, logic, or the quest for theoretical systems. The Greeks wondered at the human condition, taking for granted that our experience tells us something about our world. Philosophy was a way of trying to understand experience, confident that, through repeated and concentrated effort, our reflections on experience could provide an ever-deepening awareness of our world and of ourselves. Unlike ancient poetry and religion, ancient philosophy was democratic; it was a habit of mind within the capacity of every human being of normal intelligence. Everyone was potentially a philosopher. Priests and poets, on the other hand, were privileged exceptions, blessed with special knowledge by the power of their relationship to the gods.

A humility and ordinariness exist in the Greek philosophical attitude that make philosophy congenial to those who do not have a taste for the narrowness and inaccessibility of today's philosophical discourse. The attitude of the Greek philosophers was (and as they originated the term and the discipline of philosophy, philosophy *ought* to mean this) simply: A deep understanding of our world will emerge if we start to reflect on different interpretations of life, put forward as different individuals converse about the why's and wherefore's of experience. Greek philosophy takes up questions as they naturally arise; it tests interpretations for their reasonableness, without prejudgment about what counts as the truth (an attitude idealized in the example of Socrates). It does not put forward preconceived theories. Ideas and arguments about what things *are* are only as good as the experiences and evidences that support them. Greek philosophers take up issues, problems, puzzles, mysteries, one by one. Ancient philosophy is something that unfolds naturally from philosophical endeavors. It is not a planned, theoretical, or systematizing program. As a result, Greek philosophy does not have the same conditions for success and failure as modern thought. It does not stand, or fall, on systems.

Instead of imposing a set of preconceived, theoretical problems for philosophers to debate, Greek philosophy emerges out of the efforts of intelligent people struck by wonder to reflect upon questions that present themselves to common-sense experience. Again, this approach points to the "democratic" quality of Greek philosophy. Physical experience of our world and the human condition is common to everybody. Because physical experience is philosophy's natural starting place, to some extent everybody can become a philosopher. Philosophy does not begin by using technical or specialized information. It starts with ordinary physical experience, the "experiential furniture" of the common world of space-time. Philosophy begins with information everybody already has from common-sense experience. Unlike physical scientists and technicians, philosophers need nothing more for their craft than what is already available to them in ordinary experience.

The genius of this philosophy is that it is anchored in common sense, but since that expression is rather general, the following passage from Mortimer Adler's book *Aristotle for Everybody* supplies helpful specifics:

> The things we share are common. There are many things that different groups of people share. There are fewer things that we all share and are common to all of us, simply because we are all human. It is in this last, all-embracing sense of the word "common" that I refer to common experiences and common notions, or common sense, as common.
>
> Our common-sense notions are expressed by such words as "thing," "body," "mind," "change," "cause," "part," "whole," "one," "many," and so on. Most of us have been using these words and notions for a long time—since we were quite young. We started to use them in order to talk about experiences that all of us have had—of things moving or remaining at rest, of plants growing, of animals being born and dying, of sitting down and getting up, of aches and pains, of going to sleep, dreaming, and waking up, of feeding and exercising our bodies, and of making up our minds.[1]

One phrase that stands out for me in this passage is "since we were quite young." Most of us have employed such an expression—an apt one for those of us interested in elementary education. As another fine philosopher, Thomas Nagel, has put it: "If philosophy has any native home, it is in the questions of children. Their state of innocence is not after all so innocent."[2]

Philosophy starts with reflection on our common awarenesses in life, so everyone naturally inclines to engage in philosophical reflection, although it may be unrefined, undeveloped, and unspecified. Regardless, philosophical reflection does not originate in some remote subject that belongs only to the few. It originates whenever thoughtful people converse about their physical world and sense their wondrous

[1] Mortimer J. Adler, *Aristotle for Everybody* (New York: Macmillan, 1978), pp. xii-xiii.
[2] Thomas Nagel, *What Does It All Mean?* (New York: Oxford University Press, 1987), p. 11.

relationship to it. As Adler says, "philosophy is everybody's business." As a way of explicating our common awarenesses of life, philosophy benefits everyone. Formal training in philosophy is worthwhile so as to *deepen* and *refine* our wonder and wisdom.

Accordingly, a sound philosophy is more like an invitation to fellow pilgrims than a call for disciples.[3] The image of the pilgrim is appropriate. Every pilgrim knows that the start of the journey may be easy, but any journey will involve challenge and adventure. One who has read the Greek philosophers knows that, while their starting point may be common sense and available to all, their common sense becomes quickly sophisticated. Again, Dr. Adler cautions the pilgrim with this succinct passage:

> Aristotle's thinking *began* with common sense, but it did not *end* there. It went much further. It added to and surrounded common sense with insights and understandings that are not common at all. His understanding of things goes deeper than ours and sometimes soars higher. It is, in a word, *uncommon* common sense.[4]

But pilgrims know that if they remain on the right path they will reach the destination promised, one that has *uncommon* worth.

The philosophy to which I refer has an ancient pedigree. There is no need to apologize for its antiquity. It is perennial philosophy (*philosophia perennis*) and has the power to speak to our world just as it spoke to Plato's and Aristotle's Athenian world in the fourth century B.C. Philosophies that pump the lifeblood of truth are not static. They furnish a wisdom that can adapt and furnish supple, adaptable rules for every succeeding generation of people. Jacques Maritain put the matter aptly: "The philosophy that is not ancient is very soon old."[5]

These preliminary comments lead us now to consider the nature of "Catholic philosophy," which developed, historically considered, as the Catholic Church absorbed ancient philosophy to beget Christian wisdom.

---

[3] For a clever discussion of the discussion of philosophical discipleship versus pilgrimage, see T. W. Johnson, *Discipleship or Pilgrimage? The Educator's Quest for Philosophy* (Albany, N.Y.: State University of New York Press, 1995).

[4] Adler, pp. xiii–xiv.

[5] Jacques Maritain, *Thomas: Conversations with a Sage*, trans. Frank Sheed (New York: Sheed & Ward, 1933), p. 58.

In the Catholic tradition, we often refer to the legacy of Greek wisdom as "perennial philosophy." It is a philosophy so fundamental that it can speak the truth to all people, regardless of time, place, culture, creed. A compelling exposition of this philosophy appears in the 1998 encyclical of Pope John Paul II, *Fides et Ratio (Faith and Reason)*:

> Although times change and knowledge increases, it is possible to discern a core of philosophical insight within the history of thought as a whole. Consider, for example, the principles of non-contradiction, finality and causality, as well as the concept of the person as a free and intelligent subject with the capacity to know God, truth and goodness. Consider as well certain fundamental moral norms which are shared by all. These are among the indications that behind different schools of thought there exists a body of knowledge which may be judged a kind of spiritual heritage of humanity. It is as if we had come upon an implicit philosophy, as a result of which all feel that they possess these principles, albeit in a general and unreflective way. Precisely because it is shared in some measure by all, this knowledge should serve as a kind of reference point for the different philosophical schools . . . .
>
> On her part, the Church cannot but set great value upon reason's drive to attain goals which render people's lives ever more worthy. She sees in philosophy the way to come to know fundamental truths about human life. At the same time, the Church considers philosophy an indispensable help for a deeper understanding of faith and for communicating the truth of the Gospel to those who do not yet know it.[6]

The Pope is saying that to be human is to be a philosophical animal. He observes, also, that this fact has theological implications. Because the power of human reason is universal to people, the Church understood early that human reason could assist in evangelization. Except for a few dissenting voices, the Church has consistently maintained that faith needs philosophical reason just as human reason needs faith. No need exists to presume hostility between faith and philosophical reason. This attitude is corroborated in Scripture (for example, Romans 1:20) and is defensible besides. For no revelation could exist unless it consisted of

[6] Pope John Paul II, *Fides et Ratio* (The Vatican: September 14, 1998), nos. 4–5; official English text available at www.vatican.va/edocs/ENG0206/_P2.HTM.

truths disclosed to rational minds, intellects capable of understanding at least the significance of Revelation.

Faith, then, actually depends on natural human reason. St. Thomas Aquinas observed that where natural reason is diminished, so is supernatural faith. As a kind of natural human reasoning, philosophy is crucial for helping supernatural faith retain its integrity and vitality for the individual and culture. The relationship between philosophical reason and faith is supportive, constructive, and thoroughly Catholic. Natural human reason and philosophy are enduring ways of knowing that can contribute to every generation's effort to find the truth.

Philosophy could provide a threefold service of interpreting Scripture, explicating articles of faith, and preparing an apologetic (a defense of Christianity to those who would dismiss it as irrational or as superstitious).

There is irony in the Church's sympathetic attitude toward philosophy. Greek religion never accepted philosophy, because the democratic spirit of philosophical inquiry threatened the status quo, the cultural power enjoyed by priests and poets. Christianity did for the Greek philosophers something Greek religion did not do: accept philosophy and make it a member of its own cultural family. When this happened, Greek wisdom was modulated and taken up into a different key. The result was no longer philosophy, but Christian theology, use of faith-inspired human reason to interpret, explain, and defend the Faith. As St. Thomas Aquinas put it: The water of philosophy had been converted into the wine of theology.

In light of this history, "Catholic philosophy" represents the use of supernaturally infused, philosophical human reason as applied to the task of defending the Christian *worldview*. Catholic philosophy is a synthesis of truth realized when previously unaided human reason (the intelligence of autonomous philosophy) is put into the service of Revelation, which, when accepted by a person, stamps the intellect with the aid of divine grace. Catholic philosophy, therefore, is no mere body of doctrine, or of dry propositions. It is a living faith-filled habit of mind, whereby our natural human intelligence, now assisted by the virtues of divine grace, has power to deepen its penetration into reality, the human condition, and the demands of conscience.

Many scholars, educators, and Catholic leaders state that Catholic schools are distinctive in their aim to "educate the whole person." One benefit of a Catholic philosophy of elementary education is that it can explicate the criteria, means, and ends involved in holistic education.

Such a philosophy exists, indeed, even though it has become harder to find in universities, including Catholic universities. This Catholic philosophical tradition is the key for elementary-school educators to "open up" what is involved in teaching students in the light of a Catholic wisdom, and also help them defend it against those who find Catholic wisdom well-intentioned error or even sheer superstition.

FOR DISCUSSION

1. Why is it a mistake to think that philosophy is logic?
2. Why is a philosophical point of view always implicit in theories of elementary education?
3. What is the nature of wonder?
4. Are there some things about which all human beings tend to wonder? If so, what are they?
5. What are definitions? How do definitions differ from arguments?
6. What do we mean by "giving an explanation"?
7. What is a question?
8. Can we ask "real" questions if we have no knowledge?
9. "Socrates said that the unexamined life is not worth living. Erasmus believed that, for the masses, the examined life is no better. As applied to Catholic schools, with whom of the two do you agree, and why?"[7]
10. "Instead of wasting time and effort in discussing philosophies of education, why not simply try things out, and if they work, just use them without being troubled about underlying philosophies?"[8] Do you agree or disagree with this statement? Why?

---

[7] Asked by Harold A. Buetow, *The Catholic School: Its Roots, Identity, and Future* (New York: Crossroad, 1988), p. 19.

[8] Ibid.

CHAPTER TWO

The Aims of Catholic Elementary Education

One cannot talk about Catholic education without speaking of its goals—theological, intellectual, and moral goals. They apply particularly to elementary education because the elementary teacher is a responsible adult whose purpose is to assist parents to direct the child toward these goals. These goals or objectives need to be identified and considered in some detail, because a tendency exists to be too vague or too specific in discussion of the goals of Catholic education. If a philosopher suspects that a subject has been treated vaguely, or narrowly or broadly, he is right to bring that to our attention. Philosophy attempts to do justice to all that a subject requires.

Today we hear about "educating the whole person," so often that the phrase has become something of a cliché. Clichés are appealing because they generally say something true. If we were to measure education by the highest conceivable standard—if we were to aspire to a *true* education—we would look for one that develops human life in the fullness of its capacities. Catholic schooling is distinctive because it can attain that standard. It rests on a truth about the human person, a truth radiating out of the Gospel, paying the human condition the compliment of being many things at once: (1) a union of body and soul, a "spirit-in-the world"; (2) a creature possessing an intellect and will, whereby it is stamped with the image of God; (3) a being of conscience, called to a moral destiny; (4) a creature who is social by nature, whose own identity is tied in some way to the identities and lives of others; (5) someone God desires to save, a creature whose happiness ultimately depends on ordering its life around the things of God.

The Gospels furnish a summary vision of all the capacities that make us fully human, exemplified most perfectly by the life of Jesus. A crucial task of a Catholic philosophy of elementary education is to explicate the criteria, means, and ends that this holistic education involves. An obvious way to accomplish this task is to read with children stories conveying how some people are admirable human beings in their own right and noble in God's eyes.

When we reflect upon the aims of Catholic education, we might be tempted to think that, as the Gospel message of salvation and our relationship to God is crucial, the identity and distinctiveness of Catholic education lies only in religious instruction. In other words, the tendency might be to think that a Catholic school and a secular (or state) school do not really differ except for religious instruction. Speaking of the Catholic identity of Catholic schools, Jerome Porath formulates two questions: "Is what is 'Catholic' about the schools their religious formation and the 'school part' just the vehicle for this faith formation? Is there anything 'Catholic' about the rest of the curriculum and programming in Catholic schools?"[1]

Those who reduce the distinctiveness of a Catholic school to faith-formation alone are, in my judgment, not doing justice to the complex vision of the human person that the gospel presents. While it is certainly the case that the gospel message is one of redemption and salvation, it is also a message of liberation. From what does the gospel message liberate us? It liberates us from a false view of freedom, the view that the essence of freedom lies in doing whatever one wants. This is a dangerous idea of freedom, because what we want can often be unfulfilling, even self-destructive, a warning captured in D. H. Lawrence's remark that the shout of freedom "is a rattling of chains and always was."

Authentic liberation, on the other hand, is "the development of man from within, freeing him from that conditioning which would prevent him from becoming a fully integrated human being."[2] This development "from within" refers to the activation of those powers that make us distinctively human. Only the proper use of human potentialities—the intellectual, the affective, the moral, and the physical—can ensure that we actualize ourselves as human beings. If we stifle or wrongly direct our potentials, we cannot realize our human nature as an active, embodied being-in-the-world.

While our ultimate liberation certainly lies in our salvation, we have a moral duty to actualize our human powers in their own right. We do not achieve this salvation at the expense of our humanity. Salvation

[1] Jerome Porath, "Not Just Religious Formation: The Academic Character of Catholic Schools," *The Catholic Character of Catholic Schools*, ed. James Youniss, John J. Convey, and Jeffrey A. McLellan (Notre Dame, Ind.: University of Notre Dame Press, 2000), p. 222.

[2] Harold A. Buetow, *The Catholic School: Its Roots, Identity, and Future* (New York: Crossroad Publishing Co.), p. 90.

builds upon humanity. Grace does not destroy nature; it perfects it. We have a moral duty, a call of conscience, to mature our human powers in ways that respect their intrinsic constitution. After all, Catholics maintain that every human being is called to holiness. The whole human being, made in God's image, hopes for perfection by grace and salvation. Our human nature and our supernatural destiny go together; they are intertwined and complementary. The Catholic school, therefore, is Catholic even apart from its mission to provide religious instruction.

The word "liberation" is appropriate. It is in this spirit that the heart and soul of any education must be "liberal." The word "liberal" comes from the Latin word *liberare*, to make free. But no freedom worthy of the name is self-defeating or destructive. True freedom is masterful, not enslaving. As Catholic philosophy understands it, true liberation

> requires the criterion of truth and a right relationship to the will of others. Truth and justice are therefore the measure of true freedom. By discarding this foundation and taking himself for God, man . . . instead of realizing himself . . . destroys himself. . . .
>
> Freedom is not the liberty to do anything whatsoever. It is the freedom to do good, and in this alone happiness is to be found.
>
> But the Gospel also concerns liberation, the development of all our human powers. It aims to make us holy, but also to make us human![3]

Blessed with this philosophical outlook, the Catholic school has the power to educate the child in the ways of being fully human, taking into account that part of what makes us completely human is our relationship to God, for which reason we were created. Catholic schooling is distinctive in its ability to educate the whole person. It rests on a distinctive philosophy of the human person that can address the requirements for both our natural and our supernatural perfection. It cannot flourish or even survive without this understanding of the human person. As religious formation expressly addresses the latter, the rest of the educational mission of the Catholic school can attend to the former, always understanding that we cannot compartmentalize these two aspects of the school. The success of each will be manifest in the unitary life of a human being.

---

[3] Ibid., p. 91.

The child has a moral right to this education, the fullness of instruction that is the distinctive charism of the Catholic elementary school. But education requires a stable culture to provide it. Moreover, a culture is a tradition of good habits, virtues, and goals that we perpetuate from generation to generation. This perpetuation takes place through human persons. The formation of culture and its transmission are part of what makes us human, a truth Jacques Maritain explained in his book *Integral Humanism*:

> Let us say that civilisation or culture is that flowering which gives space for a rightly human life; is concerned not only with the necessary material development which permits the leading of a proper life here below, but also and primarily with men's moral development, the development of those spiritual and practical (artistic and ethical) activities which rightly merit the name of human progress. Civilisation is thus seen to be a natural thing in the same sense as are the workings of reason and virtue, whose fruit and accomplishment it is.[4]

"Civilization" and "culture," then, are alternative words for "education"; for it is by means of education that culture is transmitted to posterity. Education civilizes. Catholic education is the way Catholic culture develops and transmits its vision of truth, morality, and the human condition.

Maritain went on to defend Catholic culture as the seed bed for cultivating the whole person, "a fully integrated human being." Education as a civilizing or enculturating endeavor produces a whole or *integral* person. Others have reiterated Maritain's vision. For example, *The Catholic School*, a document produced by the Sacred Congregation for Catholic Education (1977), states:

> A close examination of the various definitions of school, and of new educational trends at every level, leads one to formulate the concept of school as a place of integral formation by means of a systematic and critical assimilation of culture. A school is, therefore, a privileged place in which, through a living encounter with a cultural inheritance, integral education occurs.[5]

---

[4] Jacques Maritain, *Integral Humanism* (London: Geoffrey Bles, 1938), p. 88.
[5] Cited in Porath, "Not Just Religious Formation," p. 228.

This same document specifies that one requirement for promoting an integral education is that educators be equipped with a worldview, "the presentation of all human learning and experience as a unified whole."

> She [the Church] establishes her own schools because she considers them as a privileged means of promoting the formation of the whole man, since the school is a center in which a specific concept of the world, of man, and of history is developed and conveyed.[6]

A worldview articulates a vision of the nature, purpose, and meaning of human life. To justify this vision of the human situation, a worldview first tries to explain comprehensively the world into which the human person is born. Always implicit in a worldview is a claim about what things actually are. What is the universe that human beings inhabit? Does it include anything supernatural? Is there a God? Do human beings possess immortal souls? Worldviews divide as they respond to these questions. For example, atheism advances a worldview contrary to Christianity. Atheists and Christians differ in their accounts of reality. The atheist asserts that the universe is godless, while the Christian believes in God. The Christian believes that God is the Creator and is personally concerned for our lives.

Our conception of the meaning of human life will be influenced by our conclusions regarding reality's nature. If we are convinced that atheism is false and that a supernatural reality exists—that the "universe is haunted," as Dallas Willard puts it—then our view of the human situation is bound to be personally and practically affected by that conviction. Furthermore, our judgment about whether or not God exists, and whether or not God is providential, is bound to have consequences regarding our beliefs about moral obligations and about the nature of the arts and sciences. For instance, a Christian believes: that human beings are a special creation of a personal God; that human beings, because possessing immaterial souls, can escape the determinism of physics and exercise free will; that human freedom burdens human beings with moral judgment; and that human beings will eventually answer to God for the moral quality of their conduct. The reality of the human condition compounded by its moral requirements gives

[6] Ibid., p. 230.

a depth and motivation to moral experience that an alternative world-view might not supply.

To address other aspects of the significance of human life, a world-view also explains political experience and the significance of history. We are social creatures. As a result, our moral lives include others, so that we must take into account the good of communities. According to Christianity, human beings by our choices and actions work out the social and historical meanings of our lives, a social experience and history that can be fully measured only by the judgment of God at the end of time.

These considerations show that the "Christian worldview" encompasses many issues, which someone not sympathetic with that world-view may find controversial. Still, a long tradition exists in Catholic philosophy which argues that we can defend the Christian worldview and show it to be at least reasonable, even to people who might not accept it. At any rate, when *The Catholic School* speaks of the school as being "a center in which a specific concept of the world, of man, and of history is developed and conveyed," it expresses the conviction that Catholic education radiates out of the Christian worldview. In other words, implicit in the Catholic worldview are the *aims* of Catholic education: knowledge of what is real; elucidation of what makes us human; judgment about how we ought to live, individually and communally; and explanation of how we human beings through own choices and actions cooperate with God's intentions for history.

These are general aims. There are at least four specific philosophical aspects that might well be considered further.

1. Knowledge of what is real

Today, we commonly think of something as real in two ways. First, the "real" refers to something mind-independent, in the external world, the world outside our ideas and imaginings, the *extra-mental* world of things. Confident that the human mind can contact the external world, Catholic schooling acquaints the student with the different ways of knowing, so that the student can know diverse things in God's creation.

Second, the "real" refers to a thing's significance or value. According to this meaning, when we are in contact with the real, we know some sort of perfection. Because something is different from nothing *because it is actual*, its actuality gives it the perfection of existence. This existential perfection is the ground of all other perfections. And because, according to Catholic teaching, only God can create something out of nothing, God is Existential Perfection Itself. To know God, then, is to know what is most actual and, thereby, perfect, or "most real."

So, broadly speaking, a primary aim of Catholic education is to convey knowledge so that the students become acquainted with (a) the kinds of things that constitute the universe (God's creation), and (b) the greater or lesser perfections in the universe. All knowledge terminates in God, for God is the Creator of all things that we can know, and God is the standard of full actuality and perfection, which everything else can only approximate. Part of the task of the Catholic elementary teacher, then, is to elicit from and reinforce in the child the sense of wonder that appreciates how all things known are connected to God.

2. Knowing what makes us human

Just as Catholic education pays tribute to the *whole* human person, aiming to provide an *integral* education that develops the natural and the supernatural person, instruction and formation in faith address the supernatural mysteries central to any Catholic education. As grace perfects nature, no Catholic education can be satisfactory if it ignores those natural powers that make us human. In our aim to develop a *human being*, Catholic educators cannot neglect what makes us *naturally* human. Paying attention to these issues is no offense to our faith, nor does it "short-shrift" the things of God. For our human nature is, like our faith, a gift of God. The natural person combines with his or her supernatural relationship to God to form the complete, integral person sought in Catholic education.

What is human nature? An integrated whole consisting of many faculties and properties that give us a distinct relationship to our world: intellect, will, freedom, conscience, social obligation. These powers are human parts that depend on and are related to our embodiment, the fact that we are organic creatures, whose powers involve bodily activity. These "higher" powers distinguish embodied humans from the other embodied living creatures; the higher powers show that we are persons.

These reflections are profoundly telling for the Catholic educator. Part of the mission of being a Catholic teacher is to cultivate in students an appreciation of the person's spiritual depth, theological mystery, and moral dignity. To be a person is to be the most significant (real) thing in the universe. Our *personhood* stamps us with God's image.

A person is an incarnate spirit empowered by love and knowledge. By love and knowledge we can transcend (be other than) our physical limits. *God Himself is a Person who transcended Himself in the free, loving act of creation.* As persons made in God's image, we humans have the capacity to go beyond ourselves by knowing and loving other persons, including God. Even in our nature, an impetus to God exists, for we have a desire to know what is real and what is perfect. God is the fulfillment of such knowledge and desire. God is Actuality and Goodness, the First Truth and Absolute Perfection.

Catholic education is distinctive in the way it can celebrate the spirituality and mystery of the human person, tying together at once our natural and supernatural circumstances. Integral education results as we appreciate our place in the universe and better understand creation and the Creator.

3. Judgment about how we ought to live, individually and communally

A person is a rational entity with the power to choose. Rationality and choice are related. Because we have intelligence, we can distinguish opposites and choose between them. These choices may or may not be good, depending on how they influence self or others. Part of being human is to have a conscience, character, and moral identity. Catholic educators must understand how persons ought to live in order to develop the Catholic moral dimensions of human life. To accomplish this, they must believe that good and evil exist, and that human life should embrace the former and avoid the latter. Hence, in its effort to cultivate all the human potentials that make us human, Catholic schooling must commit to the reality of the moral good and the moral consequences of what students believe and do. Accordingly, Catholic education rejects the moral relativism common to much of secular education today, sloganized and popularized in "values-neutral" education and in "values clarification."

In addition, our social nature requires that, in developing our humanity, we must relate ourselves to others in healthy human ways. Just as I have my dignity because of rationality and choice, so others have their dignity. Respect for human dignity requires a truly human regard for others, not merely for myself; for, like me, other people are human. By this insight, we can act to take into account the real good of others. Hereby, we can limit selfish desires and appreciate the dignity of others as equal to our own. Out of this consideration, justice is born.

An integral, Catholic education, then, cannot ignore the demands of conscience, involving the formation of *individual* character and the development of true *social* justice.

4. How human beings cooperate with God's intentions for history

As St. Augustine explained centuries ago in *The City of God*, history for a Christian has a purpose. It is not simply a chronicle "of one thing after another." Christian thought revolutionized the idea of history by enriching it with divine purpose. Human beings are historically and socially situated. God eternally desires to see how human beings, in our social circumstances, at this time and place, through our choices and actions, define our character. God eternally desires to see how, with the assistance of His grace, by moral choice and conduct, we can become worthy in His eyes.

History, then, is a drama rich in moral significance. For the Christian, history is a living record of successive human experiences set up intentionally by God so as to witness and evaluate that drama. History, like time, has a beginning and an end, when God will judge its meaning and value. Time is linear, not cyclical, as was the pointless, hence ahistorical, view of time conceived by the ancient Greeks, Egyptians, Hittites, Romans, and other peoples. This revolution about time and history results from the moral and metaphysical worth Christian doctrine attaches to human events. This significance develops out of decisions made by free persons who must bear the consequences of their choices causing those events, and who will be judged by God for such choices and actions.

The full mystery of human experience gives history temporal and eternal importance. Allowing us to have our own history explains two important dimensions of Christian teaching: (1) *how* God will eventually judge who has cooperated in working out his salvation and who has failed to do so (to separate "the sheep" from "the goats," as it were), and (2) *why* God permits evil as a consequence of human choices and actions, some evils being inevitable because some free persons will choose to *be* bad and to *do* evil.

History is necessary for us to have the opportunity to work out our destinies as free agents. Christianity concerns our drama of salvation as free agents (persons) and judges the moral quality of our efforts to participate in that salvation. In recent years, theologians have called this imposition on the "children of God" (Scripture's homage to human persons, who are free and who are burdened with accountability) the challenge of "soul-making." The full measure of its significance has been concisely captured in John Hick's book *Evil and the God of Love*: "It is an ethically reasonable judgment, even though . . . not one capable of demonstrative proof, that human goodness slowly built up through personal histories of moral effort has a value in the eyes of the Creator which justifies even the long travail of the soul-making process."[7] Volumes of theology exist in this one sentence suggesting why the Christian view of history is distinctive; in it is implicit the whole of Christian teaching: from why Christ came—the Incarnation and the Atonement—to the Last Judgment, before the establishment of the New Jerusalem, where God will make all things new.

All sound Catholic education—from the elementary to the university level—embraces this Christian teaching in order to be unequivocally Catholic. In this teaching is the fullness of the mystery and value of human experience, our social nature, the requirements of moral character, God's design for salvation, and the Christian rehabilitation of history from mere chronicle to moral and metaphysical drama having supreme worth "in the eyes of the Creator." Teaching the child to appreciate that his or her life has temporal and eternal significance is at the center of Catholic education, starting at the elementary level.

DISCUSSION QUESTIONS

1. What is the view of the human person that radiates from the Gospels?
2. Was Jesus a philosopher?
3. What is education? When and where does education exist? What does education develop?
4. Given the aims of Catholic elementary education, how does the Catholic elementary school serve non-Catholics?
5. What do we mean when we call something "real"? What is the opposite of real?
6. What is a teacher? What is a student?

[7] John Hick, *Evil and the God of Love* (New York: Harper & Row, 1977), p. 255.

CHAPTER THREE

Lessons from the History of Catholic Education

Catholic education aims to guide students in the ways of Christian knowledge and wisdom. Such an endeavor was clear to early Christian educators, although for political and social reasons they sometimes had trouble separating themselves and their students from the non-Christian influences prevalent in their times. Christian educators face a similar challenge today. We must have some strategy for countering beliefs that undermine Christian education. To accomplish this, we need a philosophy, whereby we can defend Christian wisdom and test other worldviews for their reasonableness and congeniality with Christian education, or lack of thereof. If a similarity exists between the demands of earlier Christian schooling and the challenges of our own time, we will be well served to recall some of the ways earlier Christian educators, explicitly and implicitly, used a philosophy of education to accomplish their mission. What can they teach us, especially about making a school distinctively Catholic? How do they convey lessons about maintaining Catholic identity in education? Furthermore, what assumptions, methods, and aims in Catholic education have been axiomatic in the past?

For convenience, brevity, and clarity, I divide this summary of the history of Catholic education into two parts: (1) a review of Catholic education from early Christian times through the zenith of High Scholasticism in the Middle Ages; (2) a synopsis of the Catholic educational experience in the Americas, from the Spanish missions to the establishment of teaching orders of Sisters in the United States. The first part communicates how a philosophy of education interested Catholics from the earliest Christian times, and how the essential themes of Catholic educational philosophy had been worked out by the end of the Middle Ages. The second part outlines some key events specific to the American Catholic educational experience. Since contemporary Catholic educators perpetuate a culture that pioneers of American Catholic education struggled mightily to create, it is important to be reminded of their challenges and achievements.

(1)

Education in the early Church is a story about the relationship between faith and reason. From its beginning, Christian education involved philosophy, as the Church struggled with the question how pre-Christian (and even non-Christian—such as Jewish, Egyptian, Greek, and Roman) wisdom-traditions could, if at all, have a beneficial influence on Christian thought. Reflection on this question led early Christian scholars to contemplate the relationship between philosophy and theology. What can philosophy or natural human reason know that could illuminate or support the Faith? Since a complete education perfects the whole person, including natural reason and infused faith, the early Church Fathers, who were the first to inspire the formation of Christian schools, were generally favorable to the idea that classical philosophy could contribute toward making Christians literate, informed, and wise.

Their thinking about the matter was quite straightforward. Education aims to give people knowledge. The word "education" derives from the Latin *e/ex*, meaning "out of," and *ducere*, "to lead." The idea is that education leads a person away from ignorance to enlightenment or knowledge. Knowledge is another word for "truth." If we educators are to accomplish our mission, we must be aware of some truths, so we can help our students discover the same truths. Thereby, the students, with the teacher's help, actively *educe* additional knowledge, as they build on truths already grasped.

For Christian education, this mission culminates in teaching the things of God and inspiring the student to desire God. In this lies our ultimate perfection of intellect and will. This must be so because Christianity holds that God is the Author of all truth, everything knowable, because God is First Truth Itself. Moreover, God is the source of everything good because He is Perfect Goodness Itself. For the Christian, then, God is the Alpha and the Omega of education, a fact that gives the Christian knowledge and *wisdom*.

"Knowledge" refers to our awareness of things, and "wisdom" denotes our highest *understanding* of our situation. This understanding implies the ability to comprehend, the capacity to *explain* how knowledge in one area connects with other ways of knowing. For example, a wise person can explain the first reasons why moral knowledge ought to inform the law, and to explain why the civil law fails if it does not

43

conform to what our rightly formed conscience tells us what ought to be. Hence, the early Church Fathers believed that Christianity was a genuine wisdom, a comprehensive way of knowing in terms of the first and highest causes. To justify this view, they explained that Christianity could assimilate what the human mind could know about God's creation without Revelation (a way of knowing called "philosophy" in ancient Greek) and what the mind could know by the blessings of Divine Revelation. If philosophy refers to our natural understanding in terms of necessary causes—a way of knowing independent of divine assistance or revelation—and if faith refers to the grace of divine Revelation, the majority of Church Fathers concluded that the relationship of philosophy to the Christian Faith is another expression of grace completing or perfecting nature. This completion (or comprehensiveness) goes by the name "Christian philosophy" or "Christian wisdom."

Mortimer J. Adler makes the comparison this way: "Philosophy at its own twin summits in metaphysics and ethics confers upon mankind a modicum of theoretical and practical wisdom, but not enough for the Christian life, either in this world or for salvation in the next. Its deficiencies must be overcome by the superior wisdom that comes only with faith."[1]

While the early Christians were animated by a pluralism and multiculturalism that made them accept as valuable the ancient pre-Christian wisdom, they still embraced pre-Christian philosophy with qualification. They reasoned that talented human beings, such as Plato and Aristotle, acquired a purely *human* wisdom. They came to know and understand many things through a rational study of causal operations, dependent on their natural reason alone, that is, independent of Divine Revelation. Philosophy, or natural reason investigating through precise causes, while *unaided* in its nature by Divine Revelation, can enter into a relationship with the grace of Christian faith. Thereby, it puts its autonomous power and achievement in the service of Christian wisdom.

Yet, wisdom is comprehensive, and the benefit rendered the human mind by the elevation to supernatural truths through the power of God's grace in Revelation goes beyond, and thus completes, natural reason. Christian faith complements and fulfills all wisdom by giving us an understanding of higher causes at work in creation. It is not at

[1] Mortimer J. Adler, *A Guidebook to Learning* (New York: Macmillan Publishing Co., 1986), p. 49.

loggerheads with other wisdom-traditions, to the extent they are true, because God is First Truth. As noted in the first chapter, this is the point made by Pope John Paul II in his encyclical *Fides et Ratio* (*Faith and Reason*): Because wisdom is a grasp of the truth and God is the source of all truth, truth's source makes no difference. All truth is "God-friendly," as it were.

We live in an age sometimes doubtful about the mind's ability to grasp the truth and suspicious of the idea that religion has any place in education. Words like "truth" and "goodness" sound curiously old-fashioned and suggest that we believe we have the right to make judgments. The hallmark of relativism is that we should make no judgments. "No judgments!" is the current catchphrase. But from the earliest Christian times, educators knew that, for many reasons, this relativism is unconvincing. Suffice it to state the most obvious: Relativism is self-refuting. When I say *No judgments!* I have made a judgment—precisely what I forbid others to do. What makes me so special that I may judge and nobody else can?

Sometimes we hear this attitude expressed in the high tones of the skeptic, who declares that the mind is inadequate to know anything. If truth is knowledge (the correspondence of the mind with actual things), and if, as the skeptic maintains, no such correspondence exists, then the skeptic asserts that no truth exists. But self-refutation again rears its head. "[O]ne cannot assert that there is no such thing as truth without contradicting oneself. If the statement that expresses the skeptic's view about truth is one that he himself regards as true, then at least one statement is true. If it is false, then it is quite possible for many other statements to be either true or false. If the statement that expresses the skeptic's view is neither true nor false, then why should we pay attention to what he says?" [2]

In light of their self-refuting nature, relativism and skepticism have not traditionally had serious play in Catholic approaches to learning. Since its beginnings, Catholic education has expressed confidence that the human mind, even a pagan or atheistic mind, however limited and humble its powers, has some capacity on its own to know truth and goodness. This attitude led early Christian writers to regard the influence of non-Christian wisdom-traditions as constructive on grounds that reason and faith should be partners, not enemies, in a student's

[2] Ibid., p. 34.

formation. Faith and reason enjoy mutual support. Confidence in this harmony proved to be the foundation of *Christian philosophy*.

As we discussed earlier, the Church Fathers recognized that we could put Christian philosophy in the service of faith, all in the spirit of *fides quaerens intellectum*, "faith seeking understanding." Philosophy could assist in (1) interpreting Scripture, (2) explicating articles of faith, and (3) defending the Christian faith against those who condemn it as superstitious. Philosophy's power to provide this assistance has repeatedly proved itself over the centuries, culminating in the thirteenth century in a theological synthesis (later known as "Scholasticism") whose greatest representative was St. Thomas Aquinas.

This cultural achievement was made possible by the belief that theology could be congenial toward philosophy. Again, irony exists in this state of affairs. For Christian religion was able to do something that ancient Greek religion did not. While Greek religion regarded philosophy as an enemy, Christian religion accepted it as a friend. Christian faith embraced philosophy and gave it a home in the development of Christian culture. As a result, philosophy as it was absorbed into Christian education was bound to have a transforming cultural power.

This absorption was quite apparent in the first Catholic school of note, the Catechetical School of Alexandria. St. Clement (150–219) founded this school under the inspiration of the motto *Credo ut intelligam*, "I believe in order to understand." By this expression, he affirmed that reason can contribute to faith. Rational reflection enables us to penetrate, deepen, explicate, and articulate the Faith. Hence, an important place exists for philosophical training in Catholic education. The person who believes and resists any effort to reflect philosophically is like a child in comparison to an adult. Still, while an underdeveloped and irrational faith is not desirable, no philosophy is true that does not harmonize with Revelation.[3]

Origen (185–255) was another member of the Catechetical School of Alexandria and a theologian of momentous influence in the early Church. He echoed St. Clement's belief that classical philosophy could empower the Christian to understand and better defend the Faith. Origen believed that no accident caused the New Testament to speak of Jesus as the *Logos*, a word in Greek with a rich history prior to its appearance in Scripture. For the philosophers, *logos* signified "word,"

[3] Frederick Copleston, *A History of Philosophy*, vol. 2, part 1 (Garden City, N.Y.: Image Books, 1962), p. 40–41.

"reason," or "explanation." Hence, the Word of God, Jesus Himself, had been prefigured in the Greek philosophers. Origen exploited this point to explain that Jesus is the exemplar of all creation. By Him and through Him everything is created; so Jesus, the Divine Word, is the mediator between the Father and creatures. Since every created thing is an expression of Christ's truth and goodness, by philosophically knowing things we draw closer to Jesus.

Along with representatives of the Catechetical School, several important minds emerged to defend the necessity of philosophy in the formation of Christian minds. This high regard for philosophy was encouraged by the need to defend Christianity in the public square against Gnostics, heretics, and other intellectuals who, for generations, challenged Christian doctrine. Saints Irenaeus, Hippolytus, Athanasius, and the two Gregorys (of Nazianzen and of Nyssa) were crucial early figures during this struggle.

St. Basil (d. 379) was a contemporary of the two Gregorys. He wrote a book, *Ad Adulescentes* (*To Adolescents*), in which he encouraged teachers to blend philosophy and religious instruction. He specifically recommended selecting philosophical passages from the works of Plato and Aristotle to reinforce truths expressed in Sacred Scripture. The overall effect of such an education would be perfection of the young person's intellect through philosophy and development of the same adolescent's moral judgment through faith. Together reason and faith form a powerful, ideal education.

Few thinkers have exercised greater influence on the development of Christian teaching than St. Augustine of Hippo (354–430). Augustine's *De Magistro* (*On the Teacher*) was so influential that, for centuries in the medieval university, professors were obliged to analyze and discuss it as part of their teaching duties. The book explains the commerce between the mind and things. Because of divine love, the human mind is so illumined that it is empowered to see in all things a sign of Christ's divinity and creative power. Things, thought, and language all point to Jesus' presence and power. Aware of this, the Christian instructor can always point the student toward the things of God, for the content of all we think, say, and know signifies divine truth, the *Logos*. Furthermore, according to Augustine, Christ Himself is the cause of all our knowledge, a doctrine known as "divine illumination." Our intellect is a light that illumines meanings and signs in things, but the source of that light is God's eternal light.

Augustine touches on another subject that bears on education: the relationship of Christian instruction to State citizenship. While Augustine believed that non-Christian communities could achieve some measure of justice, their justice would be partial and incomplete, and compromised by original sin. Christian justice would fulfill natural justice, and Christ's grace could enhance such a community so as to mitigate the effects of original sin. Accordingly, the Christian school must be on guard against the authority of the State to interfere in education. Christian allegiance to the State depends on whether that particular body-politic acts in accordance with God's eternal and natural law. To the extent it does not, the Christian must insulate students from the corrupting effects of a non-Christian culture and politics, teaching the students to be *in, but not of,* the world. Augustine defines a society as a "multitude of rational creatures associated in a common agreement as to the things which it loves." Only love of divine Truth can order a community into a Christian community. A Christian school, then, requires that order.

In the fifth, sixth, and seventh centuries, civilization struggled to keep its bearings in the wake of the collapse of the Roman Empire. Neither contemplatives nor activists had the opportunity to create an educational renaissance. Instead, the best and brightest educators labored to preserve, not add to, the legacy of culture. Three important Christian minds stand out during this period: BOETHIUS (480–525), who transmitted the genius of Plato and Aristotle to the Christian Middle Ages; CASSIODORUS (477–565), who summarized all knowledge according to the seven liberal arts; and ISIDORE OF SEVILLE, who compiled an encyclopedia of all existing art and science.

The work of Boethius was crucial because it employed Greek philosophy to pose and solve problems (such as whether humans are free if God knows future events) that would fascinate scholars for generations to come, especially the educators forming the first universities in the twelfth and thirteenth centuries. The work of Boethius, Cassiodorus, and Isidore of Seville—the so-called "transmitters"—proved to be of great consequence in the eighth century when Charlemagne summoned a renaissance in early medieval education.

CHARLEMAGNE wanted to end Christian Europe's wandering about in a "Dark Age," a period of decline that had lasted arguably some 150 years. Charlemagne was crowned Holy Roman Emperor on December 25, 800. Some twenty years before, however, he had set upon the task of elevating the cultural conditions of his subjects by improving education. To effect this change, he sought educational leaders. He had to import them from abroad because his own Frankish kingdom had become a cultural backwater, like much of Western Europe, conspicuously devoid of scholars and teachers. His reforms benefited from the advice of a few scholars from Italy and Germany, but they were especially assisted by the influence of the celebrated English educator ALCUIN OF YORK. York had become the leading cultural and educational center in England since the time of the VENERABLE BEDE (674–735), whose work as a historian was quite as influential as, simultaneously, his theological commentary and chronicle of important events in the late antiquity of England.

To accommodate Alcuin, Charlemagne built a "Palatine School," so named because it was a school formally associated with the king's palace. There Alcuin sought to compile a sizeable library and to assemble monks who would be exhorted to zeal for learning. Some historians maintain that some centuries later this Palatine School grew to become the University of Paris.

To give scope to the teaching vocation of the monks, Alcuin designed a curriculum of instruction. Eventually, this program expanded to include schools at the abbey of St. Martin at Tours and at the monasteries of St. Gall, Corbie, and Fulda. While Alcuin was not an original thinker, he had a gift for organizing instruction around classical learning synthesized with a Christian vision of the educated person. In a letter to the Emperor, he recounted how he served to some of his students "the honey of the Holy Scriptures, while others he tries to intoxicate with the wine of ancient literature: some are nourished on the apples of grammatical studies, while to others he displays the order of the shining orbs which adorn the azure heavens. (Charlemagne had a considerable personal interest in astronomy and the two men corresponded on this subject.)" [4]

In the main, Alcuin's curriculum consisted of a general educational program with a curriculum of special studies set aside for students aiming at the priestly vocation. Students called to the priesthood were expected to spend considerable time in the study of theology and scriptural exegesis. For all students, however, an intense curriculum of studies existed in the seven liberal arts: the *trivium* (grammar, rhetoric,

[4] Ibid., p. 126.

49

and dialectic) and the *quadrivium* (arithmetic, geometry, astronomy, and music).

Study of the seven liberal arts took on more importance as medieval education matured. In one way or another, the liberal arts had been discussed as essential to education since ancient times. During the Middle Ages, however, a heightened expectation existed that students would display these seven skills, so that they could study effectively what they would be taught in faculties of theology, law, and medicine. They were "liberal" (from the Latin, *liberare*, "to set free") in that they liberated the mind from the limitations of one specialized skill or drudgery and could empower it to converse with any art or science, even the highest science, theology.

From one point of view, each liberal art is more than an art or skill— a science. Each has its own set of objects that it must know. And, while, strictly speaking, logic is an art, not a science, because logicians use rationally derived principles, definitions, distinctions, and axioms to study laws of human reasoning, *analogously* we sometimes extend the term "science" to these arts. Strictly speaking, however, logic and the other six liberal arts are arts: "operational skills," virtues of the mind, that enable us to become conversant with any intellectual discipline. "As arts, they provide us with intellectual know-how."[5] Hence, they are "fundamentals" that educators can expect their students to command as they advance in their studies.

As medieval Catholic schools increasingly taught the liberal arts, students became more competent in the way they applied their skills in the development of philosophical expertise. This improvement had significant results in producing better theologians, not to mention better lawyers and physicians. Two important schools emerged in the twelfth century that pulled students beyond the liberal arts toward cultivating sophisticated philosophical and theological studies: the Schools of Chartres and St. Victor. These "monastic" or "cathedral" schools were the distant beginnings of the medieval universities, out of which later emerged the present-day university system.

These schools numbered famous thinkers, such as Peter Abelard, Hugh of St. Victor, and John of Salisbury, who philosophically debated many subjects, drawing heavily on Plato, Aristotle, and the Stoics. John discussed how Roman law could apply to medieval Christendom in

[5] Mortimer J. Adler, *A Guidebook to Learning*, p. 50.

such a way as to explain the best relationship between secular power and the papacy. His work was eventful because this would become an important subject as secular princes moved to assert their authority over the Church in the centuries to come.

The monastic and cathedral schools prepared the way for the great medieval universities, the first of which was founded at Bologna in 1150. Many important centers of learning followed, especially in France and Spain, while England and Germany waited another century before formally giving charters to their universities, Oxford, Cambridge, and Cologne. But Seville and Salamanca had already been chartered by the middle of the thirteenth century. The University of Paris received its formal statutes in 1215 and soon became the greatest intellectual center in western Europe.

A development of singular importance at the University of Paris was the work of St. Thomas Aquinas, a distinguished Master of Theology, who later was designated a Doctor of the Church. St. Thomas's influence in Catholic education largely lay in his effort to articulate better than anyone before him the right of philosophy to contribute to Christian wisdom. He observed that theologians had become content to offer little more than commentary on Scripture and the teachings of past Church authorities, such as the Fathers of the Church.

While St. Thomas did not reject this method, he saw that theologians, empowered by philosophy, could go beyond it. His "procedure was first to accept, as presuppositions, conclusions of others, the magisterial Church, and then, to proceed according to reasoned arguments from first principles derived through abstraction by natural reason from sensation."[6] Some authorities in the Church at the time had not been educated in philosophy and misunderstood St. Thomas's efforts. "In seeking to put philosophy to use within theology, St. Thomas had to defend his practice against the charge that he was mixing the wine of Revelation with the water of philosophy. St. Thomas's famous reply was that he was not mixing philosophy with Revelation but transforming the watery substance of philosophy into the wine of theology."[7]

St. Thomas's *De Magistro* (*The Teacher*—titled the same as Augustine's earlier treatise) comments on the teacher's craft in a way that is especially relevant to elementary education. In this book, St. Thomas

---

[6] Peter Redpath, *Wisdom's Odyssey: From Philosophy to Transcendental Sophistry* (Amsterdam, The Netherlands: Editions Rodopi, B.V., 1997), p. 58.

[7] Ibid., p. 59.

explains that education is of little value if the teacher cannot translate what he or she knows into practice. St. Thomas understands that, while education depends upon contemplation, a powerful component of action must exist in the teacher's craft, a point of view that is very much in concert with the ideal of the Dominican Order, to which St. Thomas belonged.

"Contemplation in action" is a Dominican motto. But what is the activity that teaching involves? While effective teaching must rely on all the liberal arts, it is no liberal art nor any sum of them. Teaching is a *cooperative*, not a liberal, art. In this regard it is like the arts of farming and healing, arts that depend on nature and the nurturing of potentialities in nature to produce their ends. This family relationship of teaching to the other cooperative arts inspires St. Thomas to employ an analogy. In *De Magistro*, he compares the teacher to a physician. (Note that the word *doctor*, in Latin, means teacher. So, the word properly applies to the teaching profession. Only later and analogously did physicians become "doctors.") The teacher aims to perfect the life of the mind so that the student can think independently, acquire truth as she or he matures, and make intelligent moral judgments. This is why the seven liberal arts are crucial. They prepare for independence of thought.

This independence of mind is supposed to liberate human nature. Education is about realizing our human potentialities. Education perfects the whole person by developing the student's capacities as a rational animal.

As rational animals, are we not already equipped to actualize our potentialities without the need of a teacher? Here St. Thomas strikes his analogy with the physician. While it is true that the human organism can sometimes recover health without the intervention of a physician, as a rule it is certainly advisable to benefit from a physician's consultation. But a capable physician knows that healing can take place only so long as the healer cooperates with the biological nature of the patient.

Likewise, we can exercise reason in life without a teacher, but our learning powers are more likely to be successfully developed if we are blessed by the guidance of teachers. Just as the physician must cooperate with the tendencies of the patient's nature to restore health, so the teacher must cooperate with human nature to perfect it. Unless educators have sufficient knowledge about how to cooperate in the actualization of the cognitive and affective powers of human nature, they cannot accomplish the goals in the art of teaching. It logically follows that sound education is essentially connected with a sound philosophy of the human person. This truth is foundational to Catholic education and is echoed through the centuries, from the time of St. Thomas Aquinas to the present.

(2)

I turn now to the history of Catholic education and the influence of Catholic schools in the New World.

In the sixteenth century, Spanish and Portuguese explorers had circumnavigated the globe. One result of this exploration was to spread Catholic culture. Shortly after the Spaniards and Portuguese started to settle in America, they opened schools, emphasizing, not surprisingly, the *trivium*: logic, grammar, and rhetoric. Before long, colonists had an ambition to create a university. Only thirty years after the founding of the first capital city in the Americas, La Española, one of its settlers, Hernando Gorjón, willed all his possessions to educated clergy who founded, upon his death, the College of Santo Domingo. This school provided instruction in the *trivium, quadrivium,* and specialized sciences besides, such as navigation, agronomy, and animal husbandry. In 1538, this institution received the title of university and was thus entitled to award degrees with the same privileges as degrees from Salamanca and Alcalá in Spain.[8]

The attitude of the Church was maternal toward all universities, as the remarks of Pope Sixtus in his apostolic constitution *Immensa* (written in 1588) indicated: "We will do everything we can not only for the University of Oxford, which we esteem greatly, but for every university, which we will heed with the love of the heart of a mother."[9] Presumably this maternalism extended to the universities of the New World.

The impact of Catholic education in the New World was swift and certain. A most remarkable story is the work of missionaries who, in colonial times, participated in a 250-year endeavor to bring Christianity

[8] Milton M. Azevedo and Kathryn K. McMahon, Editors, *Lecturas Periodisticas* (Lexington, Mass.: D. C. Heath and Company), p. 18.

[9] Translated by Ronald J. Nuzzi in "Selected Church Documents: The Organization of Centralized Authority," in *Handbook of Research on Catholic Education*, ed. Thomas C. Hunt, Ellis A. Joseph, and Ronald J. Nuzzi (Westport, Conn.: Greenwood Press, 2001), p. 6.

to a continent that is now Mexico, the United States, and Canada. "The hardship and deprivation suffered by these priests were extraordinary, but they persisted because they believed they were doing God's work in a new territory uncorrupted by sin." [10]

A brief summary of "important moments in the history of American Catholic education" is provided by the Reverend Peter M. J. Stravinskas:

> The first school within the territorial expanse of what is now the United States was a Catholic school, established by the Franciscans in Florida in 1606. The opening of schools in all the Spanish territories was a pattern followed in California and New Mexico as the Franciscans sought to educate the children of both the colonists and the native Americans.
>
> The French exploration of the New World led to the opening of the first school for boys in New Orleans in 1722 by a Capuchin friar; the Ursuline nuns began a girls' school in that city five years later. These schools became prototypes of those to spring up along the St. Lawrence River and in St. Louis, Kaskaskia, Mackinaw, Detroit, Vincennes and Maine (where a Catholic school existed as early as 1640). [11]

Spanish missionaries first brought efforts at conversion and education to the southern part of what is now known as the United States by Spanish missionaries. The Spanish government devised what became known as the "mission system," whose aim was to pacify, and subsequently train, the native populations to serve the interests of Spanish colonial expansion, using the generally altruistic motives of the missionaries for their purposes.

The mission brought a cultural revolution to the New World. Missionaries sought to reach the minds and souls of children. They baptized children first and set up schools to give them specific religious instruction. The chapel provided a classroom; memorizing Scripture and reciting stories about the Holy Family, the Apostles, and the lives of the saints were common assignments. "Missionaries were men of great faith, and to a man they believed that simple efforts would lead to

---

[10] Timothy Walch, *Parish School: American Catholic Parochial Education from Colonial Times to the Present* (New York: Crossroad Publishing Company, 1996), p. 7.

[11] Peter M. J. Stravinskas, *Constitutional Rights and Religious Prejudice: Catholic Education as the Battleground* (Milwaukee: Catholic League for Religious and Civil Rights, 1982), p. 18.

lifelong conversion." [12] As the generations rolled along, wholesale conversion had taken place through the missions.

One benefit of the mission was that it provided vocational training to assist native populations in making their daily lives better. In this way, the mission provided more than religious instruction, everything from sewing and weaving to farming and cattle-ranching. It empowered people to civilize the frontier.

In spite of their promising beginnings, by 1700, missions in Florida, Texas and New Mexico had closed. Inconsistent leadership made difficult the ability to keep lines of communication and supplies available. Native revolts, unfavorable political decisions in Spain, and threats from the British contributed to instability in the Florida missions. Elsewhere "enslavement of Native Americans and their subsequent rebellion undermined the New Mexico missions, and Texas was a lost cause almost from the start. The church had little impact on these regions before the eighteenth century." [13]

The story of the westernmost missions is a story of two special leaders: the Italian Jesuit EUSEBIO KINO, who established missions among the Pima Indians in Arizona, and JUNIPERO SERRA, a Franciscan, who set up nine missions along the coast from San Diego to San Francisco. While the Arizona missions thrived during the life of Father Kino, they showed no vitality after his death. They started to fade away with his own passing in 1711.

The California missions were most successful because Serra was a man of practical abilities who had the foresight to put in charge effective leaders at the different outposts. These missions were also blessed by the California climate and topography. These made vocational and agrarian efforts more likely to succeed. Additionally, the Native Americans in California were more congenial to the missionaries. For these reasons, the California missions thrived well into the nineteenth century. A combination of killing off, by hard labor, the native populations in the production of beef, wine, and fruit and the eventual influx of miners for gold spelled the end of mission culture in California. [14]

The accomplishments of French missionaries, especially the Jesuit "black robes," in Canada and in the northern parts of the central and eastern United States were remarkable in the seventeenth century. Like

[12] Ibid., p. 9.
[13] Ibid.
[14] Ibid., p. 10.

the strategy of the Spanish missionaries, French educational methods aimed at converting and instructing children. Afterward, the objective was to convert tribal leaders so that the remaining tribal members would follow. While the Spanish had mixed success, the fledgling French religious schools were generally failures, although a report exists that "fire and brimstone" tactics had some effect. "When it came to persuading the Indians to accept Christianity, no better technique could be used than to instill in them a fear of eternal damnation." [15]

As with Fathers Kino and Serra, success of the French missions largely depended on the leadership, commitment, and endurance of holy men. "The self-sacrifice of priests such as Jean de Brébeuf, Gabriel Lalemant, René Menard, and Isaac Jogues was legendary. These men literally devoted their lives to a valiant but vain effort to convert the Huron, the Algonquin, and even the Iroquois to Catholicism." [16] Jogues was killed by the Iroquois in 1646. Brébeuf and Lalemant suffered at the hands of the Iroquois in 1649, when their mission in a Huron village was overrun. The two priests were summarily tortured, mutilated, burned, and eventually eaten by the Iroquois, a passion that ranks among the most horrifying in the records of martyrdom.

Their deaths chilled the excitement of French missionary ambitions. Few priests subsequently were as heroic or as adventuresome as the North American martyrs. "Succeeding generations of French priests did not migrate to the New World in equivalent numbers, and those who did travel to Quebec worked among the natives who had already been converted to Catholicism." [17] By 1749, only nineteen Jesuits remained in mission work in all of North America. The French and Indian War (1754–1763) between the French and English and the suppression of the Society of Jesus by the pope in 1763 brought to an end the French missionary effort in the United States.

We might wonder whether Catholic interests improved as English dominance displaced French influence on the continent. Catholics, it turns out, faced a slow, uphill march in gaining acceptance from the English colonists in America. "By 1765, there were only about twenty-five thousand Catholics in the English colonies out of an estimated population of nearly two million." [18] But a small population was not the

---

[15] Jay Dolan, *The American Catholic Experience* (Garden City, N.Y.: Doubleday, 1985), p. 52.
[16] Walch, *Parish School*, p. 11.
[17] Ibid., p. 12.
[18] Ibid.

chief reason for the marginalization of Catholics in America. An anti-Catholicism existed in the English tradition "that was codified into law in the years between 1690 and 1776. In Massachusetts, for example, Catholics were prohibited from holding religious services, preaching Catholic doctrine, or organizing their own congregations. In Maryland, Catholics were denied the right to vote, to practice law, or to hold public office.... Only in Pennsylvania and Rhode Island—two colonies founded by religious dissenters—did Catholics have any measure of religious freedom."[19]

Obviously, in such a climate, Catholics retreated into their own culture. As a result, Catholic children were largely taught at home. But Jesuit activity existed in Maryland even in the seventeenth century, and a school, Newton Manor, opened there in 1640. A century later, another Catholic school opened in Maryland in Cecil County. This school became known as "Bohemia Manor" and had as a distinguished alumnus John Carroll, who became the first Catholic bishop in America. These successes were counterbalanced by Catholic school closings in Baltimore in 1757. In 1774, a Catholic school in the same city was attacked by an angry mob.

As citizens found a common identity opposing the British, the Revolution eased tensions against Catholics. "State legislatures in the 1770s dropped legal restrictions keeping Catholics from full citizenship and added statutes on the freedom of conscience and religion. Pennsylvania passed such laws in September 1776, and Maryland followed in November with a constitution that eliminated all restrictions on the practice of Catholicism. Catholics responded by fighting for independence side by side with their Protestant compatriots."[20]

It is only natural that Catholics would do so. The doctrine of unalienable rights, stated by Jefferson in the *Declaration of Independence*, and the Bill of Rights, laid out in the first ten articles of the Constitution, are perfectly consonant with the Catholic commitment to the philosophical doctrine of natural law. According to this moral philosophy, which has its roots in the ancient philosophers, and which has been passed down to posterity through Catholic writers, such as St. Thomas Aquinas, a just society is one that enables human life to flourish. Tyranny is condemned because it prevents human beings from fulfilling their natural duty to pursue happiness. This duty essentially

[19] Ibid., p. 13.
[20] Ibid., p. 15.

involves perfecting our human potentials. These undeveloped potentials are basic needs which, if left unfulfilled, prevent us from living a
happy human life. These potentials or needs are the basis of human
rights. Vatican Council II's *Gaudium et Spes* (*Pastoral Constitution on the
Church in the Modern World*) echoes this natural-law doctrine:

> Therefore, there must be made available to all men everything
> necessary for leading a life truly human, such as food, clothing,
> and shelter; the right to choose a state of life freely and to found
> a family, the right to education, to employment, to a good reputa-
> tion, to respect, to appropriate information, to activity in accord
> with the upright norm of one's own conscience, to protection of
> privacy and rightful freedom even in matters religious.[21]

Contrary to some popular prejudice, Catholicism is not at odds with
the spirit of true American democracy. "All Catholic-school goals are
consonant with the foundational principles of the United States. The
historian Henry Steele Commager said that 'after 1880 it might indeed
be maintained that the Catholic Church was one of the most effective of
all agencies for democracy and Americanization.' "[22] During the Revolutionary War, therefore, Catholics could in good conscience fight
alongside Protestants for the same political ideals.

As tensions relaxed between the Protestant majority and the Catholic population, many Catholics enjoyed their new peace and security in
the United States. In time, assimilation became attractive. Catholics
wanted to fit into and be accepted by the dominant Protestant culture.
This desire provoked an alarm among the Catholic authorities, including Bishop John Carroll of Baltimore:

> Carroll's initial campaign for parish schools was motivated by a
> simple concern. Without Catholic schools or some similar social
> institution, untold numbers of Catholics would be lost to the
> Church through intermarriage and what Carroll called "unavoid-
> able intercourses with non-Catholics." In his first pastoral letter to

[21] Jerome Porath, "Not Just Religious Formation: The Academic Character of Catholic Schools," *The Catholic Character of Catholic Schools*, ed. James Youniss, John J. Convey, and Jeffrey A. McLellan (Notre Dame, Ind.: University of Notre Dame Press, 2000), p. 227.
[22] Harold A. Buetow, *The Catholic School: Its Roots, Identity, and Future* (New York: Crossroad Publishing Co., 1988), p. 78.

the American Church in 1792, Carroll emphasized the importance of Christian education as a means of instilling principles that would preserve religious faith. He called on parents to educate their children while they retained "their native docility and their hearts are uncorrupted by vice." [23]

The influx of immigrants expanded the Catholic population and re-inforced the common belief among the Protestant population that Catholicism was a European religion and an anti-American cultural force. Sometimes tensions escalated again between the Catholic and non-Catholic populations. Keeping Catholic children secure and edu-cating them in the ways of Catholic faith and culture became a twofold objective among Catholic educators in the first few decades of the nineteenth century. Instrumental in this task were religious orders of Sisters, whose influence on the development of American Catholic education we cannot overestimate.

JEAN CHEVERUS, the first bishop of Boston, established a parish school in 1820, with four Ursuline Sisters providing the instruction. Unfortunately, within a few years, three of these four Sisters died of consumption. The school could not meet the needs of the large Irish Catholic population in Boston.

The promise of parish schools in America was aided substantially by the single-minded determination of ELIZABETH BAYLEY SETON, a humble convert to Catholicism who after her death was named the first native-born American saint. Seton's vision of an order of teaching Sisters and their subsequent hard work and sacrifice stimulated the appeal and the effectiveness of parish schools in the United States. "Staffing no fewer than fifteen schools in eleven cities in the years between 1809 and 1830, Seton's Sisters of Charity brought stability and order to an otherwise chaotic pattern of Catholic educational develop-ment between success and failure in many Catholic parishes. It was an extraordinary achievement—even for an American saint." [24]

After some nomadic years on the East Coast and in Europe, Eliza-beth Ann Seton finally settled in the Maryland community of Emmits-burg. "Along the way, Seton suffered the death of her husband, converted to Catholicism, was shunned by her family, and established a

[23] Walch, *Parish School,* p. 16.
[24] Ibid., p. 20.

59

Catholic school in Baltimore. Her journey ended when she established the American branch of the Daughters of Charity. The motherhouse at Emmitsburg became the nerve center of a national educational enterprise." [25]

Seton took seriously the Catholic school as an effective way for the Church to serve the world. Part of her genius was to recognize that the relative absence of parish schools was a vacuum waiting to be filled. She saw that nothing was really standing in her way, for the Church had no internal bureaucratic structures that paid attention to parish schools. "Seminaries were the original concern of church officials, followed by universities. Only recently did Catholic schools below the university level receive any solicitude." [26] She took the major cities by storm, where she especially established schools for orphans and the poor.

> She sent three Sisters to Philadelphia in 1814 to open St. Joseph's orphan asylum and sent four Sisters to New York three years later to establish a similar institution. Seton Sisters would go on to establish asylums in Baltimore and Frederick, Maryland; Washington, D.C.; Harrisburg, Pennsylvania; Albany, New York; Cincinnati, Ohio; Wilmington, Delaware; and New Orleans, Louisiana, during the 1820's. More importantly, most of these asylums doubled as the first formal schools for Catholic children in those communities. Elizabeth Seton earned her reputation as the founder of the Catholic parochial school movement in the United States. [27]

The era of teaching Sisters has brought us to the threshold of the present experience in parish schools. After Vatican Council II, many priests and nuns left the consecrated life. Today, the laity are asked to serve in Catholic schools in ways provided by priests and nuns in the past. (I am hopeful the decades ahead will show that this transition is bearing good fruit.}

Specific themes emerge in this brief overview of Catholic education. First was the challenge educators undertook to relate faith to reason. Ancient and medieval Christian educators understood that teaching was a cooperative art requiring a philosophy of the human person so as

---

[25] Ibid.
[26] Ronald J. Nuzzi, "Selected Church Documents," p. 24.
[27] Walch, *Parish School*, pp. 20–21.

to specify the student's potentialities, the actualization of which constitute education. This education had as its ultimate aim and fulfillment the beatific vision.

In America, a long struggle existed to clear away barriers to the establishment of Catholic schools. In colonial America, the existence of Catholicism, let alone Catholic schools, was tenuous. After the Revolutionary War, Americans accepted that Catholic populations were a permanent reality. But this attitude was tested when Protestant Americans became alarmed by the influx of thousands of Catholic immigrants from Europe. In response, Catholic culture put itself in a defensive posture, seeking to preserve and protect its religious identity from a Protestant America that was often hostile. The parish school was a way of insulating Catholic children from outside threats to their faith. Bishop Carroll and his fellow Catholics struggled to keep up with the demand for parish schools. Their record was mixed at best.

Congregations of Sisters played a crucial role in successfully establishing and proliferating parish schools. "The hard work and persistence of Elizabeth Seton and other women like her led to a steady supply of devoted Sister-teachers who were the backbone of the parish school system for nearly 125 years."[28] The theme of self-sacrifice is emphasized by Timothy Walch:

> Yet the most important theme—one that pervades the history of Catholic education from its earliest days—is sacrifice. For more than two centuries, Catholics from many nations and a wide range of professions were willing to risk their personal safety for the greater glory of God. To be sure, some of these Catholics were motivated by the hope of personal gain. Yet one cannot dispute that most colonial Catholics—missionaries and colonists alike— were willing to sacrifice their well-being for the sake of education. They all knew that the future of the Church in the New World was tied to educating the next generation in the ways of the Faith. It was a goal worthy of personal sacrifice.[29]

A temptation exists to think that because we live today in an affluent America in which Catholics have been assimilated into American culture, demands of sacrifice no longer exist. Such thinking is a dangerous

[28] Ibid.
[29] Ibid., pp. 21–22.

mistake. Students today, even very young minds, are bombarded with influences that undermine a Catholic education. They are subjected to influences by elements in our culture that are transforming Western society into a post-Christian civilization. Students are influenced, and perhaps even assaulted, by alternative, non-Christian, even anti-Christian, worldviews. For these reasons, the burden of sacrifice on Catholic educators is profound. They, like Catholic parents, seek ways to protect and somewhat insulate the student from the destructive forces of anti-Christian culture. We must be able to do this in addition to acquiring sufficient awareness about the Catholic philosophy of the human person to educate a young mind in human and Catholic ways of knowing and wisdom. Provided we take the risk of martyrdom out of the equation, the challenge before Catholic educators today is analogous to, and perhaps just as daunting as, the demands of Christian education in earlier times.

There are two aspects of the Catholic educator's task, one positive, one negative. Every Catholic educator needs a sound philosophy of the human person to help realize the student's cognitive and affective potentialities. And each teacher needs sufficient awareness of Catholic philosophy to diagnose and criticize doctrines, arguments, and convictions intrinsic to non-Catholic, even anti-Catholic, worldviews. Without these two abilities, Catholic education will become enfeebled and will lose a battle of attrition against opposing worldviews.

The positive dimension of Catholic elementary education is the focus of the next two chapters. The negative occupies our attention in the last chapter.

FOR DISCUSSION

1. How do the accomplishments of past Catholic educators influence Catholic elementary teachers today?
2. What has been the contribution of the Catholic Church to Western education?
3. What is the difference between "higher" and "lower" education?
4. What is truth? What is falsehood?
5. What is faith? What is reason? What is theology? What is philosophy?
6. What is the relationship between Catholicism and American democracy? Is Catholicism supportive of pluralism?
7. What are the liberal arts? Why are they crucial for education?

CHAPTER FOUR

The Child Is a Human Person

In an excellent book, the Reverend Harold A. Buetow expresses the aim of Catholic education by answering the question "Who ideally are the educated Catholics?" He answers:

> They are personally educated to the maximal point of their intelligence. They are morally formed to do God's will in their unique circumstances. They are free of encumbrances that might keep them from developing to their full potential. They are emotionally warm but controlled. They are sensitive to others and to the world around them. They reflect upon values, meanings, and problems. They strive for wisdom. In action, they achieve being responsible. They are firmly rooted in their family and also have durable bonds with people outside their family. They have developed the ability to love properly. They have achieved self-identity, freedom, and self-fulfillment.[1]

If these are the educated Catholics, if this is the aim or goal of Catholic education, how do we achieve this ideal? In formal terms: by a joint effort of student, teacher, Church, family, and society—to help fulfill the cognitive and behavioral potentialities of the child and adult. By developing *habits* that better an individual as a knower, as a disciplined moral agent, and as a controlled emotional creature, the student flourishes as a human being who can exercise his human powers easily and effectively. Of course, this is a process of fulfillment that is never complete, according to the teachings of the Catholic Faith, until the human person is in blessed company with the Triune God. When we appreciate this trajectory of education, then the elementary school teacher might better appreciate that he or she has a singular charge. Elementary education is crucial in putting the child on the right path to this formation.

[1] Harold A. Buetow, *The Catholic School: Its Roots, Identity, and Future* (New York: Crossroad Publishing Co., 1988), p 89.

To know a child's potentialities, we must know, first, what it is to be a human person, and second, what it is to be in constant communication with a child. Education is "correct" only when the philosophy of the human person upon which it rests is sound. Helping the human person to fulfillment is the goal of education understood in the broad sense. To this end, we must achieve many specific goals. The educator should have in-depth familiarity with the cognitive, volitional, and affective powers of the human person, and understand the crucial nature of human education as an on-going conversation.

Human knowledge, will, and emotions generally are three aspects of this process I shall consider first. Then, in the next chapter, we can examine the idea that education is essentially the formation of conversational *habits* because it is in *habituating* the activation of our specifically human teaching and learning powers that we *become* educated. Against this view stand several pseudo philosophical and pedagogical beliefs that undermine Catholic education, and these will be the focus of my concluding chapter. In this way, we can examine the *constructive* features of a Catholic philosophy of elementary education and address the *polemical* requirements of that same philosophy.

Human Knowledge

Elementary education is nothing if it does not inform the child. On the most basic level, how are we informed? (Another way of asking this is: How do we come to know things?) Clearly, this is a basic philosophical question. The nature of human knowledge—what we know and how we know—is a twofold question that is relevant to the perspective that philosophy provides.

Christian philosophers have debated questions about the nature of knowledge in ancient and medieval times; with some notable exceptions, they generally agreed that the most reasonable way to understand human knowledge is to recognize that it is an intellectual act having its source in sense experience. Aristotle's judgment that the human mind is as "a writing-tablet on which as yet nothing actually stands written" (*De Anima*, III.4, 430 a. 1–2) has inspired the often-quoted dictum that *there is nothing in the intellect that is not first in the senses*. Common sense appears to vindicate these judgments. It is difficult to imagine how anyone could ever come to know anything if, since birth, he suffered total sensory deprivation.

These observations form the basis of what philosophers call "sense-realism." "Realism" refers to the philosophical defense of most people's (including especially the ancient Greek philosophers') conviction that knowledge originates in the senses, whereby we become directly acquainted with things that exist independently or outside our minds. The content of our intellects is not produced by our mind's own internal states. It is produced by the real world of material things as we physically engage them through the powers of our sense organs.

Most educators and their students are naturally sense-realists in their attitudes about knowledge; realism is therefore a suitable way to approach the question of human knowledge, despite the fact that realism is not the fashion among the majority of contemporary philosophers, nor is it the main course in philosophical instruction at most universities. But because Catholic education has traditionally relied on realism in its educational outlook, many philosophers and educators who criticize Catholic education sometimes also, by association, criticize sense-realism.

Nevertheless, we must honestly recognize three points: (1) Everyone in the practical conduct of his or her life is a sense-realist (even the anti-realist skeptic, who is unequivocally a common-sense realist when he gets out of the way of an on-coming truck). (2) Catholic education historically has always been implicitly, if not explicitly, sense-realist in its attitudes about the possibility, nature, and formation of knowledge. (3) And we can justify sense-realism against alternative accounts of knowledge, in spite of the fact that only a minority of philosophers champion it at today's universities.

This means that when, as Catholic educators, we talk about knowledge, two tasks are set before us: an explanation of how the human person acquires knowledge, which gives direction to the specifics of elementary school instruction, and how sense-realism equips us to be on guard against educational theories and practices compromised by unsound philosophies of knowledge and of the human person.

Knowledge and the philosophy of the human person go together. What it is to be a knower largely makes evident what it is to be a human person. To put in perspective the emotional and affective aspects of human life, we need to see how they are related to ways of human knowing. Further, Catholic wisdom believes that philosophy finds its fulfillment in Christian faith. In the Catholic tradition, faith itself is a kind of knowledge, assured by acceptance of God's self-revelation.

Hence, it is difficult to overstate the significance of cognition in a Catholic philosophy of elementary education.

The Catholic Church teaches that the human person is a union of body and soul. The Catholic Faith holds that not all *persons* are so: angels and the Trinity are persons because we define a person as a rational nature with free choice and powers of intellectual communication. Only human persons, however, are *embodied* persons or incarnate spirits. A philosophy of the human person, therefore, addresses what it is to be an embodied person.

Consider now another truism: We are animals. As persons, though, we are more than animals. Schools of thought exist that would reduce the human person to merely an animal and perhaps a *wild* animal at that. (This extreme view we can address in a later chapter.) But it is certainly true that human beings are animals, and a successful philosophy of the human person must elucidate our animal nature.

We derive the word "animal" from the Latin, *anima*, meaning soul. An animal is an ensouled creature, differentiated from plants by virtue of the kind of soul it has, that which is the source of its powers of sensation and change of place. Aristotle observed that animals require the ability to move in place inasmuch as sensation is pointless if an animal cannot move toward or away from what it perceives.

One danger that arises when speaking about sensation is to regard it piecemeal or to think of it as though it is a mechanical operation not organically related to the consciousness of the human person. Another danger is to forget that sense-knowledge involves more than our five external senses—sight, sound, smell, taste, and touch; it is concerned also with *internal senses*.

To escape the first error, we observe what happens when we relate ourselves to our world. Our senses are necessary for this relationship, but our whole organism is involved as an active knower whenever sense knowledge takes place. For example, when I see a landscape or hear a concert, the whole I, the organically whole, conscious, knowing person, is seeing and hearing. Obvious enough. But in the effort to focus on the organs of sensation, philosophers and educators sometimes speak as though knowledge is organ-specific, as though activation of specific sense organs and their objects are operating independently of the rest of the person (or animal) who is conscious and knowing. This is why we would find it odd to say, "My eyes see a landscape" or "My ears hear a concert." We would make such a remark only as a matter of emphasis on one or the other sense or after a manner of speaking in an unusual context.

The whole organic person organizes and synthesizes experience into a whole. Research in neurology bears this out, as it shows that the inputs of sensation are bombardments of pluralized, atomized, electrical impulses. Yet perception attained through the action of the sensations is unitary, intelligible, and coherent. Neurology cannot explain this opposition between the pluralized impulses of the multitude of sensations and the intelligible unified nature of perception. Attempts to reduce human knowing to the operation of discrete physical organs and parts neglect the presence of perception in sense-experience.[2] As a result, sense-realism regards the senses as faculties or powers by which a conscious animal (whether nonhuman or human) becomes aware of its world. Through the physical actions of the senses in contact with physical phenomena in the world, information comes to animal consciousness, the order and intelligibility of which are made evident to a human person through abstracting activities of internal senses and the human mind.

The synthesizing and the ordering powers of the internal senses and the human mind require natural abilities and powers beyond the five external senses. Aristotle indicated that, in addition to the external senses, several *internal* senses exist. He enumerates, first, a *general sense*, a power by which we are able to sense differences between the different external senses. For example: a perceiver may *see* a cube of sugar; he may *taste* it as sweet. The general sense shares in both senses and, by so doing, enables him to recognize that the whiteness of the sugar perceived by his seeing faculty belongs to the same object whose sweetness he perceived by his power of taste. We take for granted that our continuous sensory inputs are coordinated and harmonized in this way. In reality, however, this unifying sense is a remarkable power and not reducible to another cognitive faculty.

In addition to the general sense, we have *imagination*, which retains the impressions of an object before our senses, even long after the senses are not perceiving that object.

---

[2] For illuminating discussions of the limits of neurology to explain mind–body interaction, see Sir John Eccles and Karl Popper, *The Self and Its Brain: An Argument for Interaction* (New York: Springer International, 1977); Robert Geis, *Personal Existence After Death: Reductionist Circularities and the Evidence* (Peru, Ill.: Sherwood Sugden and Co., 1995); John Searle, *Minds, Brains, and Science* (Cambridge, Mass.: Harvard University Press, 1984).

Long- and short-term *memories* are other internal faculties. These enable us to recall and order retained images in time and place. The action of these faculties is evident in our ability to combine or divide images.

Furthermore, like other higher forms of animal life, we human beings have an *estimative sense*, whereby we are able to determine by instinct or by biological inclination that something is good or bad for us. For example, by natural instinct, a lamb knows that a wolf is a danger. Likewise, the lamb knows that its mother provides security and nutrition. It knows these things without training. In the human person, this sense is weak, so much so that, while we have instincts and inclinations, we appear to lack instinctual mechanisms. For this reason, the estimative sense is present in human nature only in a weak and vestigial way. In human life, pursuit of the human good and avoidance of human evil are largely a matter of intellectual judgment, not sensory instinct. For this reason, some philosophers replace the expression "estimative sense" with "particular reason."

We are animals, and thus endowed with sensory powers, but we are also intellectual or rational animals, and thus have faculties and powers beyond our animal nature. We are animals and persons, a fact showing that we differ from the other animals in *degree* and in *kind*. This fact should keep the elementary educator on guard against reductionistic educational philosophies—often presented as social-scientific theories—that treat the human person as merely another animal.

Rational intelligence and symbolic language are uniquely human faculties. We are human *animals*. That is to say, we depend on our bodies to acquire information about our world. The senses, situated in our bodies, are the faculties by which we acquire content for our knowledge. The senses serve up information that our intellects assimilate as signs. So it must be if "there is nothing in the intellect that is not first in the senses."

How is there communication between our intellects and our senses so that our intellects have conceptual content? Apparently, we explain this by our human intellect's ability to apprehend traits common to objects known by our senses. The intellect has a special ability to focus on what traits certain things may have in common, so much so that we can ignore features that make things different. This attention to what is common, and the *indifference* to what is different in things, is an intellectual operation called "abstraction." This word derives from the Latin, *ab*, "away from," and *tractare*, "to draw." This operation, then, is aptly named, for in abstraction the intellect isolates or "draws out" of things their common and significant features and ignores characteristics which differentiate them. For example, the concept *animal* refers to organisms with powers of sensation and self-movement. By considering only these shared features, we can refer the word "animal" in the same way to many different species, from dog and shark, to bee and zebra.

Another, more sophisticated, example is mathematical knowledge. Through mathematical mental abilities, we are able, abstractly, to consider the quantities of things. Mathematical knowledge arises as a person uses the mind to focus exclusively on the discrete (countable) or continuous (extended and shaped) quantities in objects we simultaneously know through our senses. The resulting abstract judgments produce arithmetic and geometry, respectively.

The human person relies on images, derived from sense experience, to form concepts. This intimacy between intellect and imagination reveals itself in the fact that no matter how sophisticated and abstract our thinking, our ideas are always accompanied by images of one kind or another. Imagination, while an internal sense, can influence the intellect to conceive and experiment with new ideas. The imagination can inspire the activity of the intellect to abstract new ideas from images. We may describe this kind of intellectual activity as "intelligent imagining" or "imaginative intelligence." Likewise, we have "intellective memory." Whereas sense memory recalls sense images, "intellective memory" recovers the content of past thoughts.

In addition to concept-formation, the human intellect has two other powers: judgment and reasoning. Judgment relates concepts to each other by combining them through the verb *is* or by separating them by *is not*. By connecting in judgment the concepts derived from experience, we can express the existence and relations of things in the world of experience. Generally, this has to do with merely reporting that certain states of affairs obtain in the world. Most judgments report contingent facts. However, some judgments provide insight into a necessary truth. Sometimes, as we intellectually judge things, we immediately grasp their self-evident truth, a truth known when we know the meaning of the words of a proposition. For example, that a whole is greater than its parts is self-evident because, once we know the meaning of wholes and parts, which we originally derive from experience, we can reflect upon their natures, signified by the terms "whole" and "part," recognizing the necessary truth that "a whole is always greater than its parts."

Insight of this kind is crucial in education because it shows how we can judge universal and necessary truths based on experience, and it provides powerful learning experiences about our personal abilities to penetrate the world of experience and to deepen our personal understanding of things and their relationships in that world. Once we witness that kind of learning and insight by the minds of students, we can exploit important learning opportunities. Jean Piaget tells the story about a boy who, while playing marbles, discovered that no matter how he arranged his ten marbles, they always equaled the product of ten. The boy, on his own, discovered the principle of commutativity in algebra. This kind of learning, called "inductive insight," is a testimony to our mental ability to abstract reliably from necessities in experience and to judge them, and to provide opportunities for the educator to encourage discovery and reflection in a child's experience.

Classical philosophers sometimes speak of *abstraction* and *judgment* as two of the three proper acts or operations of the intellect. The third is *reasoning*. Reasoning is moving our mental focus from evidence to conclusions warranted by that evidence. The evidence and the conclusions, combined, constitute "argument" or "reasoning" (or in old-fashioned language, "syllogism"). To reason is to justify a claim to knowledge based, presumably, upon what we already know. As such, it is an essential philosophical skill for every educated person. Philosophy trains us in the art of justification. Having opinions is not good enough to constitute being an educated human being. We must be able intellectually to defend our beliefs. If an educator is not sensitive to the high standards of justification, he or she does a disservice to students. Educators must serve as models for the norms of justification for their students. Unless we are influenced by an anti-intellectual culture, we human beings are naturally and normally disposed to expect justifications—an edifying fact, indicating further that we are *philosophical animals*.

As Mortimer J. Adler liked to say, "philosophy is everybody's business," and many reasons exist to think that this is so. One argument is that some proficiency in philosophical skills renders our intellect more artful or skillful as we negotiate our way through divergent beliefs and opinions in life.

A helpful acronym for the art of intellectual reasoning is COJAC. *C* is for clarity, because it is crucial to determine the meaning of terms before defending or criticizing a belief. *O* stands for order. Philosophers try to grasp how things can or should be classified. Failure to categorize things properly is an error in logic, preventing us from correctly judging how subjects are related and from intelligently reasoning to conclusions. *J* is for justification. Philosophy is nothing if not the ability to defend our claims to knowledge, or at least to demonstrate that our opinions are rational. *A* is for analysis. One way to achieve clarity is to break down issues or problems into their component parts. Analysis, moreover, can provide information to test the adequacy of purported justifications. The final *C* refers to "challenging assumptions." This is a fundamental philosophical skill, for opinions commonly rest on other presumptive beliefs. This is key for the Catholic educator, who must be able to assay the many competing philosophical theories about education.

Sometimes, as we observed earlier, these conpeting theories are popular and a few may even enjoy the consensus of educators in the profession; and yet the individual teacher, employing philosophical proficiencies, may reasonably judge them all to be unacceptable. Of course, the burden is on that individual teacher to make his or her case, or to justify on philosophical grounds why an opinion or theory and its presumptions are unacceptable. When that takes place, we can foster a teaching culture animated by the philosophical muse.

These same skills are crucial for the elementary student. Even in the early years of schooling, the child benefits if teachers provide models for these skills. Simple enough to do. For example, a teacher, while reading a story to a child, could elicit conversation by discussing who is the most important character in a story and why; how the characters are like people she knows; what events in the story remind her of something in her own life; why she thinks the story uses some words (and not others) repeatedly; whether she could imagine the story having a different ending; and what would happen to the story if some of the characters were different?

Every good teacher knows that such questions can bring about remarkable conversations, even in very young children. These questions are ways of engaging the child in *wonder*. Under the influence of wonder, children seek philosophical understanding, which may impel them to develop skills in clarification and justification. Through such conversation, a little philosopher starts to awaken in the child. That children can be philosophical may surprise some. It comes as no surprise, however, to someone philosophizing in the spirit of the ancient Greeks. Adler's dictum that philosophy is for everybody applies to children as well.

Children start to exercise their intellect and imagination to clarify and explain experiences read or heard in a story. They invigorate intellect, imagination, and memory by relating the story to their lives. Should the story take them to unfamiliar, imaginary realms, their faculties will be challenged all the more. The alien excites the imagination. The child as a whole person, aided by a teacher so as to be emotionally engaged and motivated in learning, starts to exercise intellect, imagination, and memory, in an emotionally satisfying way, for conversational mood and method in the classroom invite each child to participate in learning.

Human Emotions and Appetites

Attraction and aversion are obviously two opposite features of animal life, for sensation is essential for animal survival and well-being. When animals know things through sense experiences, they may desire them or they may avoid them. Hence, the mother grizzly may be attracted by the scent of the stream where she knows there are trout to eat, but may nonetheless avoid the location because she also scents the presence of male grizzlies who might threaten her cubs. Because animals know their world, they can respond to it *appetitively*. Purposeful behavior, then, describes the lives of animals because of their inclinations to seek what is good for them and to avoid what is bad for them. This fact is expressed in the word "appetition," which derives from the Latin *ad-petere*, "to seek after."

It would be an oversimplification, however, to assert that pursuing what is pleasant and avoiding the unpleasant fully explains animal inclinations in response to their sense awarenesses. Animals are inclined also, and often instinctually driven, to behave in ways that involve difficulty. For the sake of survival and the pursuit of useful objectives, animals will show aggressive behavior.

On occasion the animal will either exert great effort to achieve a difficult goal or will expose itself to great danger, even risking death, in defending its territory or its young. For example, a herd of caribou will run to the point of exhaustion to escape a pack of hungry wolves; an antelope will flee from marauding lions. On occasion, too, an animal, rather than fleeing when faced with a dangerous aggressor, will itself become aggressive, stand its ground, and risk serious injury and even death. Thus a she-bear will defend its cubs against a mountain lion. It also happens that certain animals will undertake exhausting and arduous tasks in order to provide for themselves, to propagate, or to protect their own kind. Salmon will fight their way upstream against incredible odds to reach safe spawning grounds; beavers will toil endless hours constructing their dams which serve both as homes and as a defense against predators; in the fall geese will fly many thousands of miles south in search of more favorable feeding grounds. Such actions are undeniably physically demanding and are undertaken not because they are pleasurable but because they are useful or even necessary for survival of the individual animal or its group.[3]

Sensory appetition, then, has a twofold, and opposite, nature: On the one hand, it seeks the pleasant and avoids the unpleasant. Philosophers have spoken of this appetite in different ways, but in common language today we speak of it as "the pleasure drive." On the other hand, sensory appetition seeks the useful and the arduous, "whether it be to achieve a difficult objective or to ward off impending danger." This appetitive power may be spoken of as the aggressive appetite or as "the aggressive drive."

This analysis shows that a sense appetite exists in animals, including human animals. But because appetite responds to human knowing, the human person has more than sense appetite. In humans, we have "an appetitive activity corresponding to intellection." Intellective appetition, which philosophers call "willing," inclines the knower toward or away from an object known by the intellective power.

Sensory and intellective appetition show that "knowing acts are not ends in themselves. Instead, knowledge usually points to something further." As embodied knowers, we human beings relate our knowledge to change and activity in our lives. "The knowing acts of the human are . . . purposeful in that there is a clear relation between what

[3] James B. Reichmann, S.J., *Philosophy of the Human Person* (Chicago: Loyola University Press, 1985), pp. 166–167.

we experience and what we do; for our activity follows, and is dependent upon, a prior cognoscitive act."[4] But in addition to seeking after an object of sense knowing, we may seek after an object of intellectual knowing. This purposeful power is referred to as volitional or voluntary appetition—the power of willing.

Considerable controversy revolves around the nature and freedom of the human will. This controversy is classically expressed in the question, "Is the human will free or determined?" This is indeed a crucial question for philosophers, and for the contemporary elementary educator, because many educational theories openly or subtly make judgments about free will. It is a question of singular importance for the Catholic educator because Christianity states that we human beings are free and responsible for our choices and actions. The Catholic educator, therefore, must be alert to insinuations in pedagogical theory and policy that would deny or attack the Catholic belief in human freedom. In their effort to be "scientific," many educators today accept a naturalistic and deterministic view of the human person and human will.

We should not confuse science with naturalism. We can value modern physical science and its findings but recognize that science has its limits and cannot reduce the human person to a scientific quantity. The human body is an object for scientific inquiry. Beyond that, science can provide only a limited account of the human condition. Social science can make its contributions, but it must do it fully aware of the limits of scientific method.

What makes us human, in the last analysis, is something to which science can obtain only partial access. We human beings are more than the physical. Human behavior and motivation involve more than can come under the view of scientific method. To comprehend the human person, one must take into account other ways of knowing besides the scientific. For example, as mentioned earlier, if we are moral creatures, then moral ways of understanding are necessary to explain what we human beings are. And Catholics must take into account morality and God's grace, love, and design for human destiny. Morality, metaphysics, and theology are all ways of knowing that do not contradict but do, in fact, complement physical science.

Nor are these ways of knowing reducible to or eliminated by social scientific ways of knowing. What makes us social? On the one hand, we

[4] Ibid., p. 15.

are social because we are animals. The sociability of animals is indeed a suitable object of social-science inquiry. To the extent that human sociability is analogous to animal social life, social science can be quite instructive. On the other hand, because human beings are persons, and therefore more than animals, social science cannot adequately account for human social nature. To be a person is to be a rational nature with free choice. Social science cannot explain our rational nature or our free choice. Moral life is a necessary feature of human life, and moral life depends on our intellect and free choice; hence social science cannot be complete in its description of our social condition. To think otherwise is to suppose that we can capture personhood, freedom, and morality in the net of social scientific method. But they elude the techniques of mathematical observation, measurement, and experiment, and those characteristics that make us fully human are properly the subject matter of ethics, philosophy, and theology, not social science.

Failure to understand the transcendental nature of the human person has been a powerful corrosive in the intellectual formation of many teachers. A common assumption exists among them that social science has replaced the philosophy of the human person. This fallacy has had pernicious effects on American education and culture. Physical science must resign itself to being only a part, although an important part, of a comprehensive philosophy of the human person, a philosophy that provides the underpinnings for Catholic elementary education.

Teachers must challenge and escape objectionable theories of human volition. For if they accept such theories uncritically, they will compromise an important task of education: moral formation. Moral education lies in habituating the human will to make choices that cultivate a life of human virtue. The common belief that education should not address moral issues, or should be "morally neutral" or "values neutral," is one product of the common acceptance among educators that social science (allied with mechanistic physical science and philosophical naturalism) explains the human condition. The resulting worldview leaves no room for a philosophy of human volition that includes free will and morality.

The Affective

Because rational intelligence is distinctive to human beings, it is widely assumed that being human lies exclusively in the exercise of reason. But human beings are embodied spirits. Our intellects depend on our bodies for their content. Again: Nothing is in the intellect that is not first in the senses. Our intellects depend on our bodies in the origin of our knowledge and in the activities that follow upon knowledge. Moreover, the fact that images always precede and accompany our concepts and judgments further witnesses to the intimate connection between our intellects and our bodies.

A human being is a union of body and soul. If we are to situate knowledge within a sound philosophy of the human person, we must be sensitive to the interaction of body and soul at every turn. The unitive nature of the human person—the combination of body and soul—justifies Étienne Gilson's observation that the human knower senses with the intellect and intellectualizes with the senses. A disembodied human intellect does not understand things. A human will abstracted from body and soul does not desire things. A sense organ detached from the person perceives no color or sound. The human person—simultaneously body, soul, and sense—as a *whole* experiences his world coherently.

The intimacy and reciprocity of consciousness and body have special bearing on emotional life. We cannot live effectively *as human beings* without integrating our emotions with our intellect and will. An examination of emotions supplies a crucial element of a philosophy of education for the Catholic elementary teacher. How educational practices, projects, and curricula influence a child's emotional development is of key importance. We who are Catholic educators must be able to judge the value of such practices. We must be especially able to assess critically any claims about emotional development that question and dismiss Catholic aims in a child's emotional formation.

Further evidence that emotions are essential to our humanity is that we actively pursue emotional experiences in our lives. This is evident to everybody. Through pastimes and amusements, we seek out ways to educe emotion in our lives. The stimulation that comes from emotions leads us to cultivate highly developed arts so as to elicit strong feelings in experience. Young and old alike appreciate the stir and gratification of emotions. Over a lifetime, we learn to cultivate occasions for the experience of emotions, and when such occasions bear fruit, we regard them in retrospect as experiences rich in meaning.

Such occasions can range from a stimulating conversation with a friend to a memorable exhibition or performance of a work of art. In fact, no exaggeration exists in saying that we prize the fine arts because they provide ways of evoking deeply personal emotional experiences. Art and media also provide ways for us to experience the emotions vicariously. Spectacles of sport and tales of adventure also are attractive because they stimulate vicarious emotion. And for those who participate directly in athletics and in daring adventure, emotions are a powerful reason why they are attracted to the experience and invest it with meaning.

Every effective pedagogue knows that the association of pleasant or rewarding emotions with learning activities effectively reinforces retention of knowledge. Today, educators commonly emphasize the emotions in learning. Daniel Goleman and other educators observe that intellect has been historically emphasized to the neglect of emotion.[5] While there may be some philosophical problems with the fashionable idea of "emotional intelligence," the phrase is a useful reminder that, without addressing the emotional inclinations, interests, and needs of a child, education cannot take place. The teacher must interrelate with students in such a way as to elicit from them a disposition to learn. A child must emotionally connect with the classroom experience so as to desire learning. If a child resists the cultivation of positive emotional responses to classroom method and content, learning will not occur.

As Catholic teachers, then, we must resist any tendency to oversimplify the teaching task. It is not putting information into the intellect of a passive knower. It is about habituating a whole human being to desire learning so much that he or she will delight in becoming a self-learner. Because students are differently disposed emotionally to this goal of self-learning, a difference in "emotional intelligence" is discernible. "Emotional intelligence" is another way of conveying the idea that attending to children's different aptitudes and abilities—in knowledge and *emotion*—is crucial. It is another way of fulfilling the need to "differentiate" teaching and learning so as to address students' individual strengths and weaknesses.

All of these considerations indicate that emotion is associated with a complexity of things in human experience. But what precisely is an emotion? It might be helpful first to specify what emotion is not. Emotions are not our knowing acts. Emotions are not reducible to our

---

[5] Daniel Goleman, *Emotional Intelligence: Why It Can Matter More Than IQ* (New York: Bantam Books, 1995).

sense awarenesses, whether these be external or internal sensations. Emotions are intimately connected with knowledge, but to reduce the one to the other would be unreasonable, simply because "we are able to sense things without the slightest trace of an accompanying emotional experience."[6] I might perceive something with my senses without being affected emotionally. Hence, neither the sense act nor the sense object is equivalent to emotion. Nor is emotion to be identified with the act or object of the intellect. I can understand something without being emotionally moved by that knowledge. For example, I note that the Nile is the world's longest river. I report that knowledge impassibly.

None of these remarks is meant to imply that emotions occur without a reason. Emotions are not causeless phenomena. They result from an awareness of something. Barring mental illness, irrational anxieties, and neurological problems, emotions arise in response to something we come to know. If a mother, who happens to have a son or daughter serving in a war, hears a news report that troops were involved in a particular conflict in which lives were lost, she reasonably may experience fear or dread. But if she does not have that information, no reason exists for her to experience those emotions. In fact, for some time after the incident, she might not have heard the news and would proceed with her normal life. The news report, once she learns of it, would significantly alter her emotional state. And if she gets subsequent news, perhaps from e-mail or letter, that her child is well, her emotional states of fear or dread transform to joy and excited gratitude.

These remarks show that a mental awareness of a sensory or an intellectual kind is integral to emotional experience. Additionally, emotion involves a somatic or bodily component. Such somatic responses are often evident to persons noting someone's behavior during emotional excitement. Fear, for instance, induces such bodily changes as more rapid heartbeat, dilation of pupils, increased rate of breathing, tensing of muscles, and a flushing of the face. Bodily responses affected by emotion are even measurable. The polygraph, for example, exploits the assumed connection between emotional experience and bodily response. So intimate, in fact, is the body's reaction to emotion that we normally first think of typical bodily reactions—such as flight during fear; a smile during joy; a tear during sadness—whenever the subject of emotions is introduced for discussion.

[6] Reichmann, *Philosophy of the Human Person*, p. 172.

Undoubtedly, at least two fundamental components exist in emotional experience: cognitive awareness and bodily reaction. But analysis of emotions reveals a third component besides. An appetitive element is associated with emotions. An emotional response does not result from merely an awareness; it results from an awareness that conveys to us information about the desirability or undesirability of our circumstances. As we become aware of something, we judge (evaluate) whether it is pleasant or unpleasant, safe or dangerous, sad or joyful, and so on. We might be indifferent to our circumstances and evaluate them with virtually no emotive response. However, when emotion does arise, it is because we have made appetitive judgment that mediates between our awareness of our existing situation and our somatic reaction. This judgment may be relatively unintellectual and on the level of the sensory appetites. But it is necessarily there to secure the communication between the intellectual judgment and the predictable emotional response.

Accordingly, emotional experience combines three elements: the cognitive, appetitive, and somatic. Should any one of these three elements be missing, there is not really a human emotional experience. Plants do not have emotions, because they lack cognition. Angels do not have emotions, because they lack bodies. "Hence we may define an emotion as a complex, internal activity consisting of an intense, spontaneous affective and somatic response to a psychic awareness."[7] In keeping with its Latin root (*emovere*, "to move out from"), an emotion involves a bodily reaction that results from, and is initiated by, a knowing act, and is qualified by a mediating act of desire or aversion.[8]

Needless to say, a philosopher or a teacher makes a grave error to ignore the singular place of emotions in teaching, learning, and living. In emotional needs and reactions lie the complex dimensions of knowledge, will, and bodily action. A Catholic philosophy of the human person understands this, integrates these dimensions, and provides a whole education.

[7] Ibid., p. 174.
[8] Ibid.

FOR DISCUSSION

1. What elements must be present for us to have any kind of human cooperation? To achieve educational organization?
2. What do we mean when we say we sense something? What do we sense?
3. Is sensing identical with perceiving? Can we sense something without perceiving it? Can we perceive something without sensing it?
4. What do we mean when we say something or someone is "free"?
5. What does being right mean? What are rights? Duties?
6. Can we have rights without duties? Do animals have rights? Duties?
7. What is the difference between wishing and choosing?
8. What is an emotion? Are emotions identical with feelings?
9. What do we mean by "health"?
10. If no real human good or evil exists, can experiencing hope or fear ever be humanly healthy?
11. What do we mean when we call something "good"? or "evil"?

CHAPTER FIVE

To Educate Is to Habituate

William Shakespeare flattered us humans by observing that we are "infinite in faculty." He refers to our intellect and will, powers that open our experience to a profound range of actions and learning possibilities as we interact with our environment. Our capacities to learn and choose are virtually unlimited. On the other hand, our physical powers are quite limited. We possess few instincts and hardly any instinctual mechanisms. Consequently, at birth we lack physical abilities to cope with our world.

Our openness and flexibility toward our environment is in stark contrast to the lives of animals. Their instincts produce particular capacities and functions, manifest in the highly specialized anatomical features and powers of animals. As a result, what one species of animal can do, another cannot because it lacks the anatomical structure and is absolutely incapable of modifying those structures to accommodate different modes of activity.[1] Polar bears cannot adapt to the environment of pythons; pythons cannot adapt to life in the Arctic Circle. Because of their biologically pre-coded instinctual mechanisms, anatomical characteristics and behavioral inclinations, animals live in different worlds.

Nature has not endowed us humans with highly specialized instinctual abilities, so we must define and cultivate our tendencies through our own efforts. To develop skills that will ensure specific actions reliably and easily, we acquire *habits*. A habit results from the exercise of memory to employ and refine our powers in specific ways. This repetition gives us a specific ability to do something easily and readily. "People cannot spread their abilities over the whole field of action possible to them but must channel them along definite lines."[2] This

---

[1] James B. Reichmann, S.J., *Philosophy of the Human Person* (Chicago: Loyola University Press, 1985), p. 188.

[2] Austin Fagothey, *Right and Reason* (7th ed., St. Louis: C. V. Mosby Co., 1981), pp. 199–200.

definiteness gives a human life trained ability and predictability. For human beings, habits function the way instincts do for animals.

Clearly, this use of the word "habit" is stricter than sometimes occurs in popular language. We sometimes expand the word casually to include any behavior where a pattern appears to exist. This very broad use of *habit* appears in such remarks as, "She has the habit of sneezing during allergy season"; "he has the habit of sleeping late"; "he has the habit of scratching his head"; "she is habitually late for class." Over time, however, philosophers have worked out a more precise rendering of what constitute habits, to target those behaviors that reflect the development and education of our distinctive human potentials.

The word "habit" means *having*. Habits are *acquired* dispositions or qualities that modify natural human activity. Habits are inclinations we *have*, developed in our natural abilities by repeated actions. They bring new qualities to human life by enabling us to initiate specific activities in our natural abilities in controlled and purposeful ways. If we had no natures, we could have no natural abilities. And if we had no natural abilities, we could have no habits. In short, once we admit we possess habits, we have to admit we have natures.

Our intellect and will dispose us toward habits, but they are not the habits themselves. Habits are formed by imparting successive behaviors that make more definite our dispositions and aptitudes. Still, we can form habits only because we *know* some activity exists that we *desire* to perform repeatedly and successfully. For example, I must know what guitar playing *is* for me to desire to do so repeatedly, whereby I ultimately develop the habit. In addition, knowledge and appetite are involved when I am engaged in the activity to which the habit is ordered. While I am playing the guitar, I am aware that I am doing so, and I will continue to play only so long as I intend to and as I remember how to.

One scholar has called habits "operational structures," a phrase that at once expresses that habits exercise powers toward action and yet do so in a way that involves ease, consistency and purpose.[3] As an acquired operational tendency, a habit is curiously situated in its relationship to *power* and *activity*. A habit is not identical with knowledge or appetite. For we can *know* things without needing skill to do so, and we can *desire* things in a random and unproductive way. Nor is a habit

---

[3] Reichmann, *Philosophy of the Human Person*, p. 187.

identical with the activity toward which it is directed, for we retain our acquired abilities even when we are not performing those actions at a given moment. Just as we retain our powers when we are not activating them (for example, we do not lose the *capacity* to talk, kick a football, or mow the lawn because we are sleeping), so we do not lose a habit even when we are not exercising a specific skill at the time. For example, we retain music skills even though not playing an instrument or singing at a particular moment. Consequently, a habit is related to a power by giving it a limiting qualitative ability and aim (an operational, determinate structure, as it were) and is related to an activity by enabling it to occur "quickly and with comparative ease and proficiency."[4] In this light, we see that a habit *actuates* (by giving structure or form) a power within definite limits, while an activity *actuates* a habit. Accordingly, a habit is related to a power as *act* to *potency*; a habit is related to an activity as *potency* to *act*.

Through repetition and practice, memory strengthens our powers to perform actions, within definite boundaries, with ease and consistency, even with a degree of perfection, at least when compared to the original efforts. While commenting on a passage from St. Thomas Aquinas's *Summa Theologiae*, Étienne Gilson captures the development of habit formation with a compelling image:

> The active power therefore generally needs time to master completely the matter to which it is applied; as with fire which does not instantaneously consume all its inflammable material nor succeeds in setting it alight at once, but gradually deprives it of its opposing dispositions until it finally masters and assimilates it completely.[5]

This illustration indicates why we can readily distinguish between someone who has a habit and someone who does not. When a child learns to read, write, and compute, the original efforts are slow and fumbling. They lack definiteness. But in time, as habits become formed, such actions are achieved with some rapidity and facility. True, we can form bad habits. But bad habits are nonetheless actions "perfected" in their own way, even though they may not be morally good, or even

---

[4] Ibid., p. 190.
[5] Étienne Gilson, *The Philosophy of St. Thomas Aquinas* (New York: Dorset Press, 1929), p. 316.

good in the sense of what ought to be. We might describe bad habits as "perfect mistakes." A child who has formed bad habits in spelling or pronunciation is a case in point.[6]

Habits rely on memory to exploit past experience and to learn from it. "A habit is acquired by acting; you must actually do the things which you want the habit of doing."[7] This rule even applies to *motor* memory. If an athlete wants to run fast in competition, he must often run fast in practice. Through habit we make a power more powerful and provide readiness to act in future circumstances. "A habit has a special cause that brings it about: a plan or order in intellect (conceived more or less vaguely) and an impulse of the will . . . a habit is something you can use when you want to, and as long as it is a habit remains under rational control."[8] This intellectual and volitional direction is true even of motor habits. The athlete may run while thinking about something else, but her intellect and will remotely guide her behavior. She might be barely conscious of her intention to keep running, so habituated is the motor activity, but her awareness of what she is doing and her intention to continue it is, nonetheless, operative and decisive.

While a habit need not bring about moral excellence, excellence as an aim of education necessitates that the student acquire habits. True, a habit often simply "perfects" our mistakes, but one obligation of teachers and parents is to alter the negative directions of undesirable habits (vices) and to redirect them toward constructive results. This controlled change in direction ideally leads to different habits altogether, formation of *good* habits (virtues). We thereby acquire a capacity to perform definite tasks in a predictive way and to perform them well.

The ideal is to perform them well and successfully because they are genuine human excellences. To acquire the habit of being grammatical or mathematical is uniquely human and intellectually good. To learn these skills well is the responsible way to form such habits. To learn ungrammatical speech and to compute inaccurately is to fail to meet the norm of grammar and mathematics, is intellectually bad, and *ought not to be*. By nature, an educated person speaks well and calculates intelligently.

---

[6] George P. Klubertanz, S.J., *The Philosophy of Human Nature* (New York: Appleton-Century-Crofts, 1953), p. 273.

[7] Ibid., p. 275.

[8] Ibid.

Sometimes the norm of habit-formation is moral. A child could form the habit of lying and could go on lying quite well ("well" by the standards of successful liars). But lying is a *morally vicious* habit because it facilitates a behavior that ought not to be (in the moral sense). Lying involves falsehood, distrust, and injustice, all of which diminish, harm, and disorder the human intellect, will, emotions, and life itself, individually and socially.

We have a very plastic nature, malleable enough to be shaped in many ways. We can train ourselves to do good *or* bad things well. Once habits are in place, they are hard to alter, destroy, or replace. This is why parents and teachers are crucial in a child's life. We can guide the child away from bad habits and encourage the development of good ones. This guidance may have to occur over the child's protests, but because he lacks maturely developed reason, the child should not have the final say in this matter. As a rule, adults who have maturity, wider experiences, and salutary habits of their own have better power of judgment than a child.

All of us want many things. But some things may *appear* desirable when *really* they are not. Life is a negotiation of choices between things that may threaten and foster our well-being. Through our choices we should seek what we need, not merely what we want. Our wants ought to correspond to our needs. Parents and teachers are indispensable agents in training or habituating the child to discern and act on that difference. This is why some progressive educational theories, including those inspired by Jean-Jacques Rousseau and John Dewey, are, in part, detrimental to education. They ignore the fundamental need of externally imposed habit-formation in educating the child. They ignore it, subvert it, or wrongly apply it, on the (mistaken) grounds that such habit-formation does violence to the child's freedom. An intelligent philosophy of the human person, however, reveals just the opposite.[9]

As a child enhances the use of his intellect with the right adult guidance, he knows more about his world. Greater knowledge expands

[9] Rousseau and Dewey are not in principle opposed to habit formation. They oppose habits that do not arise naturally from the child's own psychological and moral constitution and experience. The development of habits under the demands, direction, and encouragement of teachers and other social authorities, they suspect, is "unenlightened" and likely to stifle the impulse toward toleration and freedom necessary for the realization of a democratic society, or "Enlightened Humanity." See also my remarks on Rousseau and Dewey in Chapter 6, below.

the horizon of his choices. Moreover, the habit of using the intellect properly enhances a child's ability to deliberate more effectively. Thus, the child is better able to distinguish between good and bad choices and to provide a rationale for such distinctions. By acquiring the habit of being "smart," the child is able to put his freedom to good use: to make good choices and to avoid bad ones.

If true freedom lies in the development of our full human nature, we can be free only when, with the help of others, we have developed our determinate human potentials. To think otherwise is to commit to the counter-intuitive belief that somehow freedom is commensurate with diminished human potentials. But our human powers cannot be developed without habituating them. Without habits, our powers are random, indeterminate, and subject to the whims of our environment; they are purposeless and fruitless. A rudderless and unproductive life cannot exemplify *human* freedom. Habits are paradoxical in that they are both limiting and liberating. Habits provide the channel, purpose, and productivity for our powers to expand the range of knowledge and action and, thus, to ensure that our choices enhance, instead of undermine, our humanity.

The correlation between habits and freedom is evident in the lives of educated people. Education enhances life by making us aware of the world's richness and complexity. By habitual knowledge, we actually become more free and adaptable, as knowledge, confidence, and skill serve us to cope with a changing world.

The Jesuit philosopher James B. Reichmann has related why failure to develop habits is more akin to slavery than to freedom:

> [A] person with few developed habits is hemmed in, as it were, by the fences of everydayness and, much like a cork bobbing on the surface of the water, is mercilessly subjected to the moods and changes of an environment that is often alien to the human mind and will. One who is uneducated in this fundamental sense, therefore, is mired in a state of immobility, as he finds all complex tasks difficult and distasteful, since they require uncommon effort to realize. Without the acquisition of operational habits, our true freedom is, in fact, actually minimized.[10]

---

[10] Reichmann, *Philosophy of the Human Person*, pp. 202–203.

Good individual habits (virtues) are crucial to us because healthy human life is largely a matter of relating means and ends. Virtues are means toward perfecting our human nature and life. Education involves more than habituating children; it involves habituating them in performance of human excellence.

Understanding this is clearly crucial for educating the Catholic child, for Catholic wisdom teaches that all our management of means and ends points toward our ultimate perfection: our right relationship with God. A Catholic formation of habits must aim toward our natural *and* supernatural perfection because we cannot be *fully and finally* perfect unless we reach the destiny for which we were created: eternal companionship with God.

Our God-given powers of cognition and appetite make us human animals. Habits are ways we have learned to put those powers to determinate and reliable use. This is why Aristotle calls a habit "a second nature, for just as nature is the principle or source of action itself, so habit is the source of facility in action."[11] Habit is an acquisition in a person, an acquired ability, added to a native power, such as knowing. For example, the habit of physical scientific inquiry involves knowledge and much more. It is a way in which we have learned with relative ease and reliability to order our knowledge by the light of the *scientific method*: good habits of observation, experimentation, and measurement. This example shows that merely to know things is not enough. Knowledge is not the same as the habit called "learning." "For this reason, people can have a lot of experience of something and still not have learned anything about it."[12] Learning refers to the refinement of our habits to such a degree that we have "an ability to identify a thing through some abstract and precise grasp of the different parts that comprise its make-up. To learn involves coming to know something by becoming abstractly familiar with the parts that make it be some one thing, and not another. Becoming *abstractly familiar* with something involves apprehending a thing with a lot of memory. As a result, people with skill tend to be familiar with the subject of their skill."[13]

This insight is significant for us because it shows, again, that education or learning is a kind of habituating in virtue, in excellent operation. When a child, say, becomes habituated in reading or mathematics or in

[11] Fagothey, *Right and Reason*, p. 199.
[12] Peter A. Redpath, *How to Read a Difficult Book* (Seattle: Galahad Books, 2004), p. 14.
[13] Ibid.

being generous or courteous, memory is embedded in the child's faculties so that these behaviors can become increasingly easier and even more agreeable.

Once the habit is formed, the child is in a position to analyze the nature of the activity to which the habit is directed. In the classroom, the teacher can provide the occasion for this abstract analysis. For example, the child can go beyond merely pronouncing the words correctly all the way to demonstrating a comprehension of what she reads. To stretch her capacity for abstract analysis, she may even be asked to *explain* what she reads. At this point, genuine learning matures habits. The child begins the sometimes long and arduous task toward refining, deepening, and mastering her habit, as becomes evident when she can intelligently discuss its nature, parts, and purpose. The child now starts to command a science, an art, a learned habit, such as chemistry or music, literature or arithmetic, morality or religion. Demonstrating that we are "abstractly familiar" in this way with acquired abilities represents a finishing or polishing of habits, a beautification process, which is the hallmark of learning.

If education is habit-forming, what kinds of educational habits, broadly understood, do we have? A habit is a further determination of our operative powers, and these fall into two general classes: *cognitive* and *appetitive*.

Cognitive Habits

A habit results from the direction or control of intellect and will. Neither our external senses nor our unifying (or "general") sense, one of the internal senses, is under the direct control of intellect and will. We cannot by a mere effort of will have an external sense experience. And we cannot control by intellect or will the way our general sense coordinates many sense impressions.

Imagination and memory, on the other hand, are internal senses that can come under the direct control of intellect and will, and therefore can be habituated. For example, we can develop the imagination to supply ourselves with images as illustrations for classroom instruction. Cultivated use of imagination is a singular skill in education. If a child cannot learn to use his imagination with agility (to stretch the imagination), the child will lack the requisite images to introduce his or her mind to new frontiers of learning. To understand mathematics, history, literature, and physical science, a child must have an imagination supple enough to think *like* (still taking into account that the child is yet only a child) a mathematician, historian, writer, poet, or astronomer.

The imagination's analogical power must be highly developed for us to be educated, a fact that must not be lost on any sound philosophy of elementary education. Analogy is a way of referring one thing to another, of indicating a relationship of unequal likeness between different things. Analogy tells us that things are alike, but are not exactly the same. It tells us that two different things unequally share in, or are related to, some third thing. For example, even though the word has the same meaning when we use it, the word *law* applies unequally to a law book, law student, or law professor because these three realities do not possess law identically.

Clearly, the mind of a child is different from that of a mature, even brilliant, adult who has perfected the habit of a specialized art or science or of drawing analogies. Nonetheless, the child's mind is a human mind empowered by imagination, the same faculty that the adult has matured. While faltering, inefficient, and underdeveloped, the child's imagination still has the capacity to form vibrant images and can begin the difficult task of learning to apply them to various arts. The child does not have the mind of Aesop, but with Aesop's help the child is able to imagine and absorb the lesson of the fable. *Analogous* or proportionate to its own level, the child's mind begins to grow in understanding and will begin to experience the delight that accompanies comprehension.

For any child to become habituated in these arts, he or she must learn to "stretch the wings" of the imagination. To challenge, strengthen, and discipline the imaginative faculty is a crucial tool toward learning to think like great minds. To ask this of children is not to dream an impossible dream. It is to pay homage to their human faculties and to assist them in their natural development.

Closely associated with imagination is the faculty of memory, without which we can have no habits at all. "Habit is embedded memory."[14] The intellect can control the memory for a particular purpose. For example, a child can memorize the multiplication table, so that he can easily solve multiplication problems. He can later delight in

[14] Ibid.

memorizing the curious names for persons, places, and things in a Harry Potter novel. He can recite them readily and enjoyably. But over and beyond simple memorization, the habit of memory can influence and structure the imagination. This influence, for instance, can create "thought experiments" that influence the habit of scientific inquiry (for example, the work of Einstein). The value of such images is that they are easier to understand than the conceptual explanation, and yet these images are signs or tools that can make the conceptual explanation available to the intellect. By reflecting on the images in the "thought experiment," we begin to think like a scientist.

So, imagination and memory are (internal) sensory powers we can and must habituate. But when we think of the most significant faculties to habituate, we turn to intellect and will, for these are the powers that make us distinctly human and scientific. Education aims to develop the whole person to inculcate wisdom and prudence. But in doing so, it must give centrality to intellectual and appetitive habits because of their primacy in human nature.

Our intellects engage the world in two ways: first, by attaining knowledge for its own sake, so as simply to be informed about things; this is knowledge (to speak in classical terms) as *contemplation*, the attainment of information as an *end* or aim; and second, by attaining knowledge not for information or observation but for its use as a *means* to *make* or *do* things; this is knowledge engaged in either production or practicality. If this is an accurate way of reflecting on intellectual knowledge, then habituation of intellectual cognition is also of two kinds: *speculative* habits (habits of contemplation); and *practical* habits (habits of making or doing). At the heart of speculative habits are (a) *science* (or demonstrative reasoning) and (b) *wisdom* (or understanding). Practical habits divide into (a) *art* and (b) *prudence*.

Speculative Habits

The Habit of Scientific Reasoning. Evident is the fact that we cannot live well without knowledge. It indicates that a basic impulse exists in human nature for knowledge. If we rob ourselves of knowledge, we cheat ourselves out of our humanity. This permits us to say that human beings *by nature* desire to know, even for its own sake. It also tells us that, by nature, we are inclined to listen to and take direction from people we think know more than we do. Hence, by nature, we are receptive to being taught. Cultivating speculative habits, then, is fundamental to our development as a human person.

The intellect seeks knowledge; and knowledge, strictly understood, is awareness of the truth. But to be totally satisfied that it has achieved its natural good, the intellect must be convinced it has attained knowledge, and not its counterfeit. The way we determine this is to rely on *evidence*, which, broadly speaking, refers either to that of which *experience* convinces us, or what *reasoning* or logic can add to experience. Combined, these two standards of evidence become the measure of conviction for the intellect to develop the *scientific habit*. To learn to think carefully is an acquired ability necessary for perfecting the intellect. The scientific habit is skill at demonstrative reasoning, a process whereby the intellect reflects on what it knows, so as to determine what logical conclusions we may necessarily derive or learn from it.

The word "scientific" in this context does not mean physical science. The word "science" derives from the Latin word, *scientia*, which means knowledge. So, the scientific habit signifies something broader than the habit of physical science. The habit developed by physical scientific inquiry is limited to the standards of the "scientific method" of physical science: good habits of observation, experimentation, and mathematical measurement. But demonstrative reasoning is not limited to this threefold method alone. As explained earlier, there are objects of human knowledge and methods of knowing, such as certain religious, metaphysical, and moral truths, that lie outside physical science. As long as it does not ignore, and is based on, experience, demonstrative reasoning can strongly support and, in some cases, justify these truths beyond a reasonable doubt. Accordingly, scientific reasoning is a broad notion: it is the habit or art of demanding evidence and right thinking for conclusions in any subject.

Scientific reasoning, thus broadly understood, tests whether the human mind has necessarily attained knowledge. In light of its assessment of the evidence, the intellect needs to determine whether it has arrived at necessary knowledge or must resign itself to some measure of doubt. When an admixture of doubt exists along with evidence for judgments, we ordinarily call such judgments "opinions." Knowledge is acceptance of something as true because of sufficient evidence that excludes opposite possibilities. Opinion, on the other hand, is acceptance of something as true without sufficient evidence. We do not reasonably doubt what we know is necessarily so. We admit doubt, however, when we think about the matter objectively, in opinion or belief. This is why we cannot logically say that we simultaneously both believe something and know it. This would be a contradictory statement because belief admits of some questioning, whereas knowledge excludes it.

The habit of scientific reasoning, then, conveys a crucial lesson of lasting value about responsible use of the human intellect. The habit of judging to what extent our intellect approximates the attainment of evidence beyond a reasonable doubt, the state of mind called "knowledge," determines whether we have a right to assert confidently a claim to knowledge or to express humbly an opinion.

Furthermore, the habit of scientific reasoning, judging according to the ultimate standard of necessary truth (of the knowledge that something can be in only one way), explains the difference between knowledge and opinion. Even when our intellects fall short of scientific knowledge and necessary truth and we must resign ourselves to mere opinion (which, unlike knowledge, is *not* an assent to the truth of something beyond a reasonable doubt), the speculative habit of demonstrative reasoning necessitates that belief be responsible. Such responsible use of the intellect presupposes that opinions be rational. Even opinions should have some evidence in their behalf. We do not have a right to believe just anything. We should not believe something just because someone wants it to be so. The habit of scientific reasoning pays homage to evidence (necessary truth) and logic. This humility before the available evidence separates the virtue (good habit) of demonstrative reasoning from wishful thinking and superstitious belief. This habit reveals the development of the "scientific attitude" and is fundamental for any educated person.

A great tragedy of modern education is the erosion of this standard of humility before the body of evidence. This is a by-product of people's despair about the possibility of knowledge because we commonly suppose that knowledge is washed away by relativism. We detect this attitude in the fashionable idea that knowledge (especially moral knowledge) is but a cultural construction. In this view, evidence and rationality become negotiable from culture to culture and from person to person; they become useful fictions. This attitude panders to the Rousseauian suspicion about external habit formation and robs the child of the right to have his or her intellect informed and ordered by the habit of true science.

The Habit of Wisdom. Wisdom, another speculative habit (or virtue), transcends knowledge by supplying understanding, the ability to justify something in light of its closest, deepest, and necessary causes. Understanding in the complete sense is taking into account nearest, deepest, and necessary causes. For that reason wisdom was traditionally defined as conversance with first or ultimate (that is, metaphysical) causes of things. In the last analysis, wisdom means understanding God as First Cause of everything. True wisdom, then, requires the habit of becoming conversant with the things of God. Highest understanding demands some awareness of how God is the first principle of the universe and of the human condition. Catholic education exists to ensure that the child begins to grasp many of the elements of the relationship of creature to God. In this way, Catholic education habituates the child in wisdom.

Practical Habits

As we exercise our intellectual power, we can become more skillful at contemplating things as they are—attainment of information as an end or aim. In other words, we develop speculative habits. But, as noted previously, speculation is not the only way the intellect operates. Our intellect may also seek knowledge for its use as a means to make or do things. This is practical knowledge. It is the habit of *artistic production.* Its perfection involves practical habits or virtues.

Another way to express the distinction between a speculative and a practical habit is that the first concerns "knowing that" or "knowing what," and the second focuses on "knowing how." Speculative investigations, such as history and the physical sciences, need to know *that* things are and *what* they are. Speculative habits concentrate on the *existence* and *natures* of things. Practical investigations limit their attention to "knowing how."

Human beings cultivate two arts of know-how. We seek to know how to *make* things. We produce objects (artworks or artifacts) that are not found in the natural world. This making also includes "performance arts," as human beings use their bodily or behavioral skills artificially (or "artfully") to communicate symbols and meanings. We also seek to know how to *act* for our own good and for the good of our communities.

The first kind of practical art is "artistic production." This is the way we most commonly use the term *art*. Art is a productive skill for making artifacts. The second kind of practical art is "prudence," the skill at how to act so as to become happy.

In the strict sense, artistic production is a habit that aims at altering something other than ourselves. Art refers to the habit of incorporating a thought or an artistic idea in some kind of matter (subject matter). It is a way of giving an external body direction, shaping it according to an artistic rule or measure. The plastic or physical arts are the best examples of art in this sense.

Analogously, *art* can refer to doing something well. Through art in this sense, we can alter ourselves. This direction is the habit of artistic practice. The fine arts, especially the "performing" arts, are examples.

In a broader sense, art directs our knowledge to improve the exercise of our faculties and judgments. This improvement cultivates the "liberal arts." They are arts because they impose operational skills on the mind. They demonstrate a facility at using symbols, meanings, words, abstractions, and numbers, so as to speak, write, behave, and demonstrate by high standards of human knowledge. Traditionally, educators demanded development of seven liberal arts: grammar, logic, and rhetoric (the *trivium* in the medieval university); music, astronomy, geometry, and arithmetic (the *quadrivium*).

Certainly, these are arts, as people demonstrate a wide range of proficiencies in their use. They are skills people bring to all learning, and some people employ them with excellence. Hence, teachers have historically sought their cultivation. They are *liberal* arts because they give the mind symbolic capacities so as to *free* it to take on ever more complex and sophisticated mental tasks.

Art uses intelligent direction to produce something. It cooperates with "matter" when it does so. Whether it is external matter (say, a sculptor's block of marble), the artist's body (say, a dancer) or "intelligible matter" (say, a logician's or poet's art), some kind of "subject matter" underlies the artist's actions. For example, the logician can demonstrate his skills only by directing the use of principles and rules. These elements are logic's subject matter (no matter how "formal" or abstract). The art of logical processes presupposes that *something* (a subject matter) is in process.

Thus, all the arts involve and cooperate with matter. Over the centuries, philosophers have spoken at length about three arts conspicuous for their cooperation with matter: farming, healing, and teaching. These arts nurture and perfect living beings. Without the cooperation of this living matter (plant, patient, or student), the artist (farmer, healer, or teacher) cannot attain his goal. While the philosophical tradition has highlighted teaching as a cooperative art, the teacher may do well to remember that all arts, in a way, are cooperative.

These comments also indicate that while arts are skills or procedures for production or action, they also involve knowledge. The arts concern objects that make them also sciences. For example, logic rests on rules, principles, and elements that are objects of knowledge. Likewise, the rhetorician can identify standard rules or causes for speaking well. Knowledge of these principles or "causes" of the art of logic or rhetoric make them also sciences. We can say the same for all the other liberal arts.

The Habit of Prudence. We need to distinguish productive art from prudence. The latter involves the art of moral choice. Prudence involves doing, in light of what is good for a human being. If ethics is the intelligent management of means and ends for human happiness, "prudence" is, in the last analysis, just another word for ethics. For prudence is skill at making intelligent choices with our happiness in view.

In guiding our conduct, prudence specifically demands these things: that we develop acute skills at analyzing and evaluating how we should act in particular, often complex, circumstances; that we order our actions to contribute to our long-term happiness, not simply our short-term good (in other words, prudence teaches that ethics is about *being* fully human, not simply about *doing*); and that we integrate our moral lives by acquiring *all* the virtues.

This last demand gives us pause. Is it not a demanding demand? Is it reasonable that we could attain all the virtues? Is it realistic to think we could eliminate every vice? Fair questions. But they only show that moral life requires a very high standard, if it is about human excellence. Prudence requires this demanding standard because it is always *imprudent* for us to let vice enter our lives. Vices are bad habits. They are bad because they undermine development of our human potentials and, ultimately, our happiness. Hence, virtue-ethics must prescribe that we acquire all the virtues. For, vice draws us to actions and things that are bad for us; virtue attracts us to actions and things that are good. The mixture of vice and virtue in life impedes integration of moral character (moral integrity). In other words, vice *disintegrates* our character. If virtue and vice pull our character in opposite directions, then admitting

95

even one vice creates disorder in our character. Our inclinations are confused and contested. Our character is in conflict with itself.

Prudence is therefore a crucial habit, and it habituates us to attain *all* good habits. It is unlikely that our natural powers are sufficient to integrate our lives perfectly, Catholic wisdom argues that we need God's grace or divine assistance to make such integration attainable. Hence, to the question "Is it reasonable to think we could eliminate every vice?" Catholicism answers, "No." But it quickly adds: "With God's help we can." Jesus was not talking only to the "natural human being" when He commanded, "Be perfect as your Father in Heaven is perfect." Once it is empowered and elevated by grace, prudence demands nothing less than a holy life. The French Catholic writer Léon Bloy captured this idea nicely: "There is only one tragedy: not to be a saint."

Appetitive Habits

Earlier I referred to two strong sensory appetites: our "pleasure drive" and our "aggressive drive." Part of the task of habit-formation is to tame, develop, and direct these drives constructively. Controlling these drives is so crucial that some ancient and Catholic philosophers have argued that human moral development depends on it. Particular habits supply this control, and these habits are those acquired perfections on which our moral development may be said *to hinge*. The Latin word for "hinge" being *cardo*, these habits came to be called "cardinal virtues." These are fundamental *moral* habits because, without them, we cannot live well or successfully.

Moderation is the moral habit that directs the pleasure drive. The tendency exists, especially among children, to think that "more is better." Without exercising self-control, we can succumb to the vice of *immoderation*. Gluttony and drunkenness are obvious examples of this vice. But it can take on "age-specific" forms, such as a child's failure to moderate his inclinations to recreation and camaraderie. A chief objective of discipline is to instill in the child the desire for moderation or self-restraint. A primary task of teachers and parents is to communicate to children that their lives will be enriched, not diminished, by the virtue of self-control. Moderation is a singular habit of self-control. It is crucial because self-control and self-moderation are necessary for developing all other habits. To convince a child that a disciplined life is a necessary condition of a happy life is perhaps the central calling of an educator.

Fortitude is the moral habit that governs the aggressive drive. As we confront adversities, if we are to live well and successfully, we must learn to persevere. The ability to sacrifice wants and interests for another goal starts the development of this moral virtue. If a child does not learn to defer gratification, he puts happiness at risk. To develop this habit and apply it intelligently, we learn to judge differences in truth and goodness. An intelligent and comprehensive view of human life, which Catholic philosophy supplies, is indispensable for empowering us to judge human action in the light of higher and lower values. To instill this judgment in a child so that he can determine what things are worth sacrifice, contest, or perseverance is another moral challenge facing us Catholic educators. Slogans like "values-neutral education" or "let children invent their own moral values" are excuses for teachers to neglect the moral requirements of integral education. Children cannot *be* educated if educators or parents do not directly contribute to their moral formation. We must make judgments daily that involve short- and long-term moral consequences. An education that does not justify the philosophical underpinnings of morality and self-consciously address moral habits (virtues) in school fails in helping children to be fully human. Because teachers are moral creatures, such an education risks the charge that they are themselves being *inhuman*.

Another appetitive virtue arises as we recognize a need to control and measure our *rational* faculty of desire, the will. Hence, in addition to the two virtues of *sense* appetite, temperance and fortitude, a virtue exists defining the *intellectual* appetite, the will. Obviously, we humans must impose a habit or control on the will, for, in itself, it is simply a faculty of desire, potentially desirous of anything we might want at any given moment. The will responds to anything that *appears* desirous to us. From the vantage point of the will, the desiring individual is the center of the universe, so to speak. Since it is purely the faculty of desire, why would it, in its own intrinsic nature, limit itself? An unbridled will simply covets objects of desire. Accordingly, the intellect must habituate the human will in a new kind of restraint. The intellect must train the will to limit and redirect its desires to include others, recognizing that other human beings with desires also exist. The intellect, accordingly, prods the will outside itself by recognizing that no human being is in this world alone. The intellect's judgment that we humans are social creatures trains the will to take into account the desires of others. The intellect imposes on the will the norm and habit of *justice*.

For Catholics, justice alone does not habituate us in our social development. Because every person is made in God's image, Catholics are called also to the virtue of *charity*. This virtue instills in us an awareness of the things of God in other creatures. A full appreciation of this fact requires grace, as the things of God in creation are a gift and a mystery. Hence, charity, unlike justice, is an *infused* (theological or supernatural), not an *acquired* (moral or cardinal), virtue.

If we add prudence to these acquired moral habits, we arrive at four cardinal virtues: prudence, temperance, fortitude, and justice. They signify norms and habits that Catholic teachers should make constitutive in the content and methods of their classroom instruction. Out of this fourfold hub, other virtues and moral standards can radiate.

Tools and Educational Methods

A distinctive way that we display our habits is in mastery of tools. Tools enable us to extend our powers in our environment. Tools extend our intentions, intelligence and bodies. Thinking of the tool as an extension of our bodies, Aristotle remarked that the human hand is "the tool of tools." This is a clever observation because it indicates, first, that tools are ways we seek to *manipulate* our world, and second, that they are designed, *purposive* ways we extend *action* in our world. "What the human hand cannot itself perform it can accomplish through the use of tools or other hands, which it fashions for itself." [15]

To master a tool, we must develop a habit. But in a way, tools themselves are habits. For the designer of a tool embeds in it his intelligence and memory. This insight further illuminates the role of the teacher as transmitter of habit-formation, because the methods a teacher uses are, as tools, ways to hold, transport, and extend information and action. If we appreciate this understanding of tools in the broad sense, we can see that anything available to us for a helpful, purposive task is rightly called "a tool."

For example, a simple list is a tool. A list intelligently orders and calls things that should be learned or accomplished. "Tools reduce the time

---

[15] Reichmann, *Philosophy of the Human Person*, p. 189.

and space that separate people from one another or from other things, save on labor, promote leisure, receive . . . and extend human knowledge." [16] In this sense, a list is as much a tool as a wrench or a car. A list saves time and space because it saves labor. It arranges items to communicate an efficient way to learn them or accomplish them. By saving time, a list provides leisure for other pursuits. As a tool for efficiently learning and doing tasks, a list fosters habits of learning and doing. And because tools convey the intentions and designs of toolmakers, all tools, including even lists, are organs of communication. A list compresses time and space, communicating how we can understand and accomplish in an orderly way. We might not have seen it in this light before, but a list really is a tool that can give direction for mastering tasks. Peter Kreeft pays tribute to lists as primitive but important instruments of communication:

> Making numbered lists . . . is the first and simplest way we learn to order "the buzzing, blooming confusion" that is our world. Children . . . and David Letterman love to make lists. Thus we find "twelve-step programs," "the Ten Commandments," "the Seven Wonders of the World," "the Five Pillars of Islam," "the Four Noble Truths," and "the Three Things More Miserable Than a Wet Chicken." To make a list is to classify many things under one general category, and at the same time to distinguish these things by assigning them different numbers. [17]

A list might seem like a "little nothing," but, in reality, it can be a powerful tool communicating the art of ordering and measuring.

These remarks indicate that we would be mistaken if we were to think of tools in a very narrow and simplistic way. Tools can include more than typical items stored in a tool box. Educators also must have tools. And as the only thing worthy of being called a "tool" is something helpful, a teacher must always consider how a tool communicates and accomplishes something good. Effective use of tools is the genius of teaching. But we must think outside the standard "toolbox" to appreciate this truth.

A book is a powerful tool at a teacher's disposal. When this tool is properly used, many things are accomplished in the habituation of

---

[16] Redpath, *How to Read a Difficult Book,* p. 9.

[17] Peter Kreeft, *Socratic Logic* (South Bend, Ind.: St. Augustine's Press, 2004), p. 1.

students. Books are tools for conversation. Through a book, an author communicates his or her intelligence and memory to a reader. A book is another instance of a tool compressing time and space; for a book is a tool that brings an author into a classroom. A book makes close at hand someone who is far away, or even dead. In the case of "great books," a book transports into the class a great mind, a great discoverer. By the power of a book, a student is able to converse with a great intellect. The teacher can facilitate this conversation so that a student begins to imagine and think like a great discoverer. The proper use of books as tools is a crucial service a teacher can render a child. To empower a child to converse effectively with great discoverers makes the book like a living teacher. The great discoverer visits the classroom as the primary teacher. The classroom teacher becomes a facilitator (another tool, in a good and helpful sense) for a child's conversation with the primary teacher. Looking at a book in this way transforms it from being dry etchings on a page, to being a living conversation (even if with a dead person!). So understood, a book is a tool for *emotionally* engaging a student and *challenging* his powers of intellect, imagination, and memory.

All learning, if it is genuine, successful, and lasting, is self-learning, and for that reason a great book is a crucial tool, for such a book provides the occasion for a child and a writer to be in intimate conversation, a conversation that could last a lifetime.

Education in the Moral Virtues

The moral virtues are habits that enable us to integrate and fulfill our determinate human potentials. As remarked earlier, attainment of moral virtues defines a human person as an excellent moral character. Moral virtues describe us as exemplary because we become the kind of human being that our human nature prescribes us to be. To attain moral virtues is excellent and morally good because it defines what we *morally ought to be*. Moral virtues refer to those habituated abilities that empower us to act in ways that perfect us; in short, to act in ways that make us happy. A human being ought to be the kind of individual and social creature who lives at his best.

Aristotle explained what "good" or "best" means here by referring to basic human potentials that, if unfulfilled, prevent us from living well and successfully as human beings. These potentials Aristotle called "real goods," as distinct from merely "apparent goods." Real goods are things human beings need. Hence, they can only be good for us, and we *ought* to acquire them. Apparent goods may or may not be really good for us, and these must be judged by whether or not they conform to real goods. Some examples of real goods are: food, clothing, shelter, health, love, friendship, intimacy, knowledge, meaningful work, self-mastery, self-esteem, playfulness, physical pleasure, spiritual meaning, security, aesthetic experience, individual freedom, and civil liberties.

These real goods are rooted in human nature, and so we have a natural right to their fulfillment; these real goods are natural, not artificial. They are not man-made privileges; they flow from our human nature. Aristotle's standard of real goods has come down to posterity in the form of "unalienable" human rights, a doctrine with which Americans are familiar, as the word appears in the Declaration of Independence and other founding documents of American government. These documents, then, echo Aristotle's virtue-ethics.

Moral virtue, accordingly, is a key element in an integral education, and something a child has a *right* to acquire. For if a child has a natural right to real goods, he has a moral right to the *means* (moral virtues) to obtain those real goods. Educating the whole child necessitates methods that instruct him in moral virtue. A chief failing of "modern" education is its unwillingness to instruct children in attaining the moral virtues. Many reasons exist for this failure, but two are conspicuous: (1) In American society, a popular prejudice exists that morality is essentially religious; separation of Church and State requires separation of morality from the classroom, unless it takes the "benign" form of "values-neutral instruction" or "values clarification." (2) In some segments of Western culture, a belief prevails that moral instruction is exclusively the business of parents; educators should not intrude on this important parental task. Sometimes this belief is put forward by educational "conservatives," who insist that education be limited to the "basics." Moral instruction belongs exclusively to parents (they say) because teachers have limited time and all of their time should be devoted to their primary duty of teaching "reading, writing, and arithmetic."

One can readily point out the error underlying these two excuses.

First, we have Aristotle's demonstration that a natural basis exists for morality. The moral virtues habituate us in living well as humans. If human nature provides a foundation for morality, we need not conclude that morality is essentially religious (derived from *supernatural* moral wisdom). Still, we know as Catholics that religious wisdom completes our moral lives. In addition to our natural or *acquired* virtues (such as the cardinal virtues), we must have the *infused* virtues (faith, hope, and charity) to work out our salvation. Human nature grounds our natural morality. Catholicism teaches that God, by special acts of creation, has produced human beings with their distinctive human natures. So, while a natural basis for morality exists, God, Who creates our human nature, also intends that we complete and transcend it by working out our supernatural destinies. As a result, Catholic education, on the one hand, objects to the claim that morality can exist only in religion. Such a claim is false because it ignores the real goods grounded in human nature that prescribe formation of our acquired moral virtues. On the other hand, Catholic education, recalling that grace perfects nature, demands that religious morality *complete* the work of education in the natural virtues. Education in the moral virtues is another testimony to the genius for whole, integral education that the Catholic school can provide.

Second, Catholic wisdom understands that parents are the primary educators of children. An effective school should be an extension of the home. Educating the whole child requires that every child be the same person undergoing moral formation by similar methods at school and home. Integral education is defeated whenever schoolroom instruction and home instruction are at loggerheads. A tragic circumstance exists whenever educators develop teaching programs (as has often occurred in the history of "progressive education") that judge parents as impediments, not as primary sources, of children's education. At its worst, a "progressive" model of teaching turns the schools into re-education camps. The idea that parents can provide little education for their children and that, at worst, they might even misguide their children's minds has been a more common attitude in American elementary education than we might comfortably admit.

True, irresponsible parents exist. In some communities they seem to abound. This is a cultural tragedy. Addressing this situation is also part of the Catholic school's mission. But it is a tragedy that we cannot remedy by assuming that the mission of the school is disconnected from the mission of the home. Teachers and families have to educate in harmony, though this is easier said than done in today's society. Still, it is an ideal that teachers and parents must strive to make real for children to achieve integral and moral education. If education is indeed for life and for the whole person, teachers, like parents, must concern themselves with the moral formation of children. Consequently, the school, especially the Catholic school, has to address more than the "three R's."

Even when teachers are motivated to provide moral instruction, they are sometimes hesitant to do so. They worry that it would entail imposing rules, litanies of "*do's* and *don't's*," on children. This reluctance is understandable because many people are unaware of a way of explaining ethics that does not reduce it to a system of rules. The idea that moral education is only about rules, precepts, commands, and prohibitions is a common misconception about morality. Fortunately, we have the wisdom of the ancient Greeks and Christians to correct that error.

As we have noted, in the traditions of ancient Greek and Catholic philosophy, philosophical morality in general and moral instruction in particular focus on how some remarkable individuals manifest human moral excellence in their lives in a striking way. This approach conforms to the Greek tendency to initiate philosophy by asking intelligent and accomplished people for reasonable explanations of experience. One obvious question is, "What is the good life?" To respond to such a question, we naturally turn to human beings conspicuous for their moral virtue, whose lives are happy, and whose judgment and conduct have enriched the lives of their families and communities. With this as our starting point, we soon see that ethics is not primarily about rules. If we make exemplary human lives our models for ethics, not parsing of rules, then we can effectively provide moral instruction without preaching or imposing abstract "rules." We need to recover this ancient perspective on morality to supply such instruction. That it is ancient is not a fault. Recall, again, Maritain's quip: "A philosophy that is not ancient is very soon old."

This perspective on moral education was natural for Catholic educators in ancient times. The Christian gospel is a lesson in virtue-ethics. To the question, "What is the good life?" the answer is, "The life of Jesus." To the question, "How should I live?" the Apostle points to Jesus and answers, "Live as He lives."

Morally excellent persons are exemplary because they exercise moral virtue, attain happiness, and manifest a plan of virtuous living. This plan might be more implicit than explicit in their lives, but it is evident nonetheless. In the past, educators have understood this principle. Much education in the past (recall the *McGuffey's Readers,* the *Bible,* and *Plutarch's Lives*) primarily emphasized examples of virtuous lives. Morally virtuous people teach us that if we follow their example, moral excellence can also be ours. The lives of admirable human beings, then, remind us that moral virtue is a human calling.

This is no mystery; if Aristotle is right that happiness is the fulfilling of our natural human powers, then only one plan of happiness exists for everyone. Since we all have the same human nature, we all have the same powers, whose fulfillment in the attainment of real goods prescribes our happiness.

Real goods, then, are the norm of everybody's happiness because everybody shares the same human nature. In fact, virtue-ethics is sometimes called "natural law" ethics, the word "natural" signifying human nature. Such language is appropriate because moral virtues are moral habits aiming to perfect human nature. Hence, moral relativism—the view that moral beliefs are merely cultural inventions (bound to vary from society to society)—is unconvincing. If we all have the same human nature, and if morality is the fulfillment of human natural powers, then we all have the same morality. Moral diversity certainly does and should exist. After all, human freedom is a real good. But human nature and real goods are the ultimate standards by which we measure the moral soundness of cultural pluralism. The evils of tyranny, child abuse, slavery, bigotry, and cultural and moral decay cannot "hide behind" cultural diversity.

For an elementary educator, an obvious way exists to provide moral instruction: reading stories and books about morally virtuous or noble lives, or (to take an indirect, contrasting approach) about the sad consequences that come from morally vicious lives. Either way, it is instruction through the method of successful (virtuous) or failed (vicious) moral examples. "It has been said that there is nothing more influential, more determinant, in a child's life than the moral power of quiet example. For children to take morality seriously they must be in the presence of adults who take morality seriously. And with their own eyes they must see adults take morality seriously." [18]

Such reading fosters literacy and promotes moral virtue. This is moral education with content, through examples. William Bennett's

[18] William J. Bennett, ed., *The Book of Virtues* (New York: Simon & Schuster, 1993), p. 11.

The Book of Virtues contains stories exemplifying virtues—self-discipline, compassion, responsibility, friendship, work, courage, perseverance, honesty, loyalty, and faith—and contains enough selections to be of interest to a range of age groups. Such a book furnishes the teacher a tool for meeting the student at his present stage of learning, and leading him from there. It does not beleaguer students with problems of "moral reasoning"; there are no debates about war, abortion, euthanasia, or animal rights, logical disputes of a sophisticated moral subject-matter for which elementary students are not yet suited. Still, students who learn the moral virtues from such stories will be better prepared later for such debates when they have learned about and have personally developed intellectual and moral habits.

Furthermore, such stories acquaint students with a history, tradition, and culture whose wisdom their integral education transmits to them. In the case of Catholic elementary education, an anthology of carefully selected moral readings can effectively transmit specific information about Catholic culture and Catholic moral wisdom.

FOR DISCUSSION

1. What do we mean when we call something "perfect" or "excellent"?
2. What do we mean by "order"? Can we have order without inequality or imperfection?
3. What is the difference between art and a work of art?
4. Can we have art without science?
5. What is a liberal art? How do liberal arts differ from mechanical arts and fine arts?
6. Can real science exist if no necessity exists?
7. What do we mean by scientific proof?
8. Can we prove anything without using definitions?
9. What is a scientific experiment? What makes an experiment "scientific"? What makes it "an experiment"?
10. Can an action be artistic but not beautiful, true, or good?
11. What is the difference between wisdom and science? Wisdom and prudence? Prudence and understanding? Science and art?
12. Can we have art without prudence?
13. Can we have art without honesty? If art in no way involves honesty, can counterfeiters exist?
14. What do we mean by ethics or morality?

15. Is human good identical with human pleasure? If so, how do we distinguish a coward from a courageous person?
16. Can wisdom or foolishness exist if no real human good exists?
17. What is human happiness?
18. What relation, if any, does education have to human happiness?

CHAPTER SIX

Confronting the Idols of the Education Tribe

Several common and virtually axiomatic opinions are asserted with earnestness and authority whenever educators gather in conversation. A large body of accepted educational dogmas exists and we are exposed to them from our earliest years as students. These dogmas have been in circulation for a long time. Most students, including those matriculating through Catholic schools, have likely come under the influence of instructors whose pedagogy is largely governed by many of these dogmas. Students having a teaching vocation are bound to encounter in their curricula at this or that university, or in this or that teacher's college, courses in which the content is driven by many of these "accepted" but erroneous educational theories. Later, when they take up residence as a professional within the teaching community, they will hear again and again the same "consensus" advocating these same dogmas.

As Catholic philosophers, we need to ask whether these axioms of education theory are acceptable in the light of the goals of Catholic education. Which of them, whether long-established or recently minted, are compatible with a philosophy of *Catholic* elementary education?

Our ability to evaluate any pedagogical ideas as to whether they are "congenial" to Catholic education is obviously crucial. Catholic educators who can discern what is congenial are able to set up "firewalls," as it were, to protect their schools from ideological influences, which would, if unchecked, spell the ruin of Catholic education. Without such barriers, our schools will be invaded by falsehood and corruption.

Some people might be uncomfortable with the idea of throwing up intellectual or cultural "firewalls." They are uneasy at words like "falsehood" and "corruption," words that smack of "judgmentalism." Is not openness, rather than separateness, really what is called for? Surely, we should not preserve Catholic identity by ignoring or retreating from the world. Such an attitude, they worry, suggests a "fortress mentality" that would effectively isolate the Catholic school from the very world it is called to serve. Then too, they might think, to insulate the Catholic school from the influences of contemporary culture would diminish the creative energies that result from engaging today's ideas and innovations; to deny the child that experience and not to sponsor that encounter directly from inside the school would rob the child of an education. That would be, they might say, ironic: The "firewall" would destroy, not preserve, Catholic education. Such a critical attitude, then, they might conclude, is exclusionary and divisive.

Such cautionary views are not to be disregarded. But a school can be open to the world while it works to preserve its identity. Still, we must not be naïve. Ideologies, attitudes, and behaviors that are incompatible with Catholic education exist. To think otherwise is to divest Catholic education of any substance. A person might find such words as "false" and "corrupt" grating, but what do we assume if we never allow them in our vocabulary? What is the alternative to permitting such judgments? The alternative would be an indifference to whatever might influence Catholic education. Any such indifference would itself be a *judgment*, a judgment not to care about how ideologies, attitudes, and behaviors might influence Catholic education. What would be the rationale for such indifference? It would be the (indefensible) idea that we could never judge anything true or false, better or worse. It would presume equivalence for all truth claims or value judgments. Pushed to its logical extreme, it would deny that a Catholic identity, distinct from other identities, religious or secular, even exists. But these are philosophical claims. So here we encounter philosophical assumptions that challenge judgments to defend the integrity—the truth and the goodness—of Catholic education.

A lesson surfaces here. In an effort to *dispense* with philosophical judgments, a person must enter the domain of the philosopher. Objection to a philosophical assumption requires philosophical argument to meet the challenge. Herein we discover something that we encounter repeatedly in talk about education theory. Any effort to set philosophy aside boomerangs. To reject philosophy is, first, to rely on philosophical assumptions and, second, to reinforce the need for a philosophical polemic. Like the fellow who tried to use logic to refute logic, philosophy is impossible to avoid. The assertion that philosophy is dispensable or irrelevant is itself a philosophical claim. Self-refutation rears its head again.

A philosophical point of view is always implicit in an educator's rationale. That was painfully obvious in some of the dogmas my colleagues expressed during that meeting I spoke of in my Preface. For example, the statement that "philosophy has been made obsolete by science" (presumably "physical science") is a philosophical assertion we can readily refute. Physical science establishes its conclusions by habits of observation, measurement, and experimentation. None of *these* methods, however, can establish the *truth* of the proposition "Philosophy has been made obsolete by physical science."

Furthermore, to define physical science and to differentiate it from other ways of knowing—such as metaphysics, ethics, and theology—is itself a philosophical endeavor. Philosophy, not physical science, debates the comprehensive question about the kinds of knowledge. Philosophy can consider all the possible ways of knowing because it can contemplate things under any mode of existence whatsoever. Even nonphysical things and negations of different kinds come under the purview of philosophy. By definition, however, they are beyond the scope of physical scientific method.

For example, a physician, speaking as a medical scientist, can describe what is involved in an operation to separate conjoined twins, but nowhere in that scientific description is there an answer to the related question, "*Should* they be separated?" A physical scientist can describe the technique and materials necessary to assemble a bacteriological weapon, but to answer whether such a weapon should ever be used is beyond the bounds of physical scientific description. Unless we are prepared to say that such questions are pointless because they are not contained in physical science, we must concede that ways of knowing exist—such as ethics—that are not reducible to physical scientific description. Other questions relevant to our grasp of reality and our appreciation of the human condition entail the same conclusion, such as whether God exists and whether human beings have immortal souls.

The judgment that physical science has replaced philosophy looks suspiciously like a conclusion someone has reached because of being impressed by a consensus among today's intelligentsia that physical science is the only genuine way of knowing. But appeal to consensus is itself another philosophical claim about knowledge that we can easily dismiss. Was it not consensus that brought us beliefs that lightning was the expression of an angry God; that the moon had no bearing on the ocean's tides; and that African-Americans were only three-fifths persons (so decided by the U.S. Supreme Court in the Dred Scott case of

1857). When it is philosophically considered, we have every right to assume that consensus is guilty until proven innocent.

An embarrassment to such a consensus is that philosophy (not physical science), because of its comprehensive perspective on reality, identifies the diverse ways of knowing, including physical science itself. Certainly, in some cases, not participating in "the consensus" is a good thing. As Mahatma Gandhi said, "You may be a voice in the wilderness, but that does not mean you are wrong."

These comments illustrate how it happens that people make philosophical statements that carry with them assumptions and implications, even though we might be loath to call those statements "philosophical." Philosophical judgments abound even when someone professes to be "anti-philosophical."

Often, philosophical assertions hide in the fashions of the social sciences. The judgment "Sex and sexuality have become far too complex and technical to leave to the typical parent" is an example of what Eric Vogelin has called the "new Gnosticism," the presumption that values and attitudes traditionally reserved for families are now the domains of technocratic elites or "experts." The idea is that someone not privy to social scientific research is not competent to guide children and adolescents on such a sensitive matter. This attitude prevailed during the heyday of progressive education (1900 to 1950), and it persists today in American education.[1]

Hence, in some school districts, parents who object to sex-education programs (to focus on but one example) are judged to be uninformed and, therefore, unsuited to debate the question. Educators and the media often characterize this disagreement by resorting to *ad hominem* accusations, judging the dispute as a collision of (say) "experts" and "fundamentalists." Instead, we should fairly (and philosophically) judge that it is a dispute between two groups who simply rely on different criteria for their positions: social scientific research *versus* the historical, experiential record of good parenting. This latter is not irrational, uninformed, or "fundamentalistic." That parents do not normally base their judgment on professional sociological research does not mean that they do not have a reasonable basis for their parenting decisions.

---

[1] For a discussion of how some elitist pedagogues have tried to marginalize the influence of parents in education, see Diane Ravitch: *Left Back: A Century of Battles over School Reform* (New York: Simon & Schuster, 2000).

In fact, parents have at least two things going for them that the experts do not. First, parents are invested in their children in such a way that, should they be negligent and irresponsible about their children's sex education, they will directly experience the negative consequences of that failure. If social scientists fail to give proper direction, they are absent when the dire consequences emerge. Likewise, many educators are enmeshed in bureaucracies that resist even the idea of failure.[2]

Social scientists and educators should not, *a priori*, dismiss parental suspicions on grounds that they are "untrained." Since social science has been, and still is, abused as a smokescreen for ideological agendas (recall how sociology, anthropology, and psychology have been used for decades to prop up moral relativism and repressive political regimes), parents have a duty to be vigilant about the danger to their children in being treated as "guinea pigs" in the service of another fashionable political or pedagogical cause.

Secondly, parents can draw on thousands of years of cultural experience and direction, especially guidance through faith, Scripture, and the Church. That some sex educators protest the reliability of such direction might speak more about the fact that sex education is ideologically driven than that it is scientifically supported.[3]

Philosophical assumptions are implicit whenever educators make assertions about what knowledge is, what criteria exist to determine child development, and what criteria exist to judge individual and social happiness. Hence, to think that philosophy is not necessarily implicit in educational rationales, programs, and practices is naïve. Philosophical assumptions exist in every educational program or practice, at least implicitly. A *worldview* (claims about truth, human nature, and morality) is implicit in those assumptions. As we observed earlier, one way to understand philosophy is to define it as a test of the reasonableness of worldviews. This purpose alone makes philosophical study a benefit to a teacher. The use of philosophical thinking and habits enables a Catholic educator the better to examine the worth of common assumptions and trends in educational theory and practice. A

[2] Thomas Sowell has interesting things to say about how some ideologies and institutions in America believe they are immune to failure; see his *The Vision of the Anointed* (New York: Basic Books, 1995).

[3] These paragraphs on sex education echo Thomas Sowell's, *Inside American Education* (New York: Free Press, 1993), chap. 3.

Catholic teacher can apply this philosophical habit inside and outside the school, thus being vigilant and armed against naïve assumptions.

As Aristotle observed, a right beginning is crucial because it determines in what direction we are headed. Just as misreading a compass can lead us on a hike to an unintended destination, so an uncritical acceptance of assumptions can lead to bad consequences for teacher and students alike. Bad philosophy leads to bad results. And this may be so even when thousands of authorities and professionals swear to the contrary. Another good definition of philosophy is relevant in this regard: the mind's check on ignorance, superstition, and arbitrary political power.[4]

Catholic education provides a genuine wisdom through a distinctive worldview, and Catholic teachers need to be intelligently selective about what philosophical views influence them.

There are many voices challenging the nature and aims specifically of Catholic elementary education. A very appropriate way of considering these challenges is in question-and-answer form.

(1) Question-and-answer is a clear and concise way of addressing an issue.

(2) Question-and-answer suggests the Greek and ancient Catholic philosophical method of reaching an intelligent position out of the natural, rational developments of a conversation between interested human beings.

(3) Challenges to Catholic education are commonly posed in the form of questions.

(4) Concise, effective answers to these questions remind the Catholic educator that, in spite of widespread belief to the contrary, the Catholic worldview (and its corresponding Catholic philosophy of education) is eminently defensible.

(5) And conversance with answers to questions challenging Catholic education habituates the Catholic elementary teacher in the arts of wisdom and demonstrative reasoning and in skills needed for defending the Catholic worldview.

I have chosen questions that are incisive and go to the heart of the Catholic worldview as related to Catholic elementary education. These questions, here presented with a brief introduction, express objections

---

[4] More than one colleague has told me that this definition is John Locke's, but I have not found it in his writings. My colleagues cannot seem to locate it, either. That Locke is the origin may be an urban legend, but it is a good definition nonetheless.

that I have heard critics of Catholicism and Catholic education repeat in diverse contexts. The replies carry implications for countless other questions as well.

Question 1. Catholic schools are not suited to educate children in the modern world because Catholicism is an authoritarian religion. As such, it is contrary to the spirit of a pluralistic education. "Values-neutral" education can instill *tolerance* in students. Tolerance is the crucial virtue for socializing students in the modern world. *So, is not "values-neutral" education superior to Catholic education in its ability to instill tolerance and thus to civilize a child for life in a world of diversity?*

Response. This question presupposes that truth and authority are incompatible with pluralism, tolerance, and multiculturalism. Nothing could be further from the truth. Catholicism might *appear* to be vulnerable to this charge of "intolerance" only because the word *tolerance* has surreptitiously changed in recent years. It has shifted from its original meaning to a relativistic meaning, which is implied in "values-neutral" methods and instruction. G. K. Chesterton noted this change several decades ago when he remarked that "today tolerance is the refuge of the person who does not believe anything."

The classical meaning of *tolerance* is found in Voltaire's famous statement, "I may disagree with what you are saying, but I will fight to the death for your right to say it." Today, however, the word has mutated into: "Disagreement is pointless because all views are equally true and valid." Disagreement itself has become a sign of *in*-tolerance.

However, if we can escape this relativizing of the word *tolerance*, we can argue that a devout Catholic could be perfectly tolerant even if he disagreed with another's worldview. This would be to employ "tolerance" in Voltaire's sense. A Catholic educator has every right to insist on this, for it is simply a prejudice to assert that "tolerance is relativism." A relativist *cannot* defend this judgment; for, if he were to try to defend it, he would need to argue that something is *more* true or valid than something else.

Relativism is the flimsiest of worldviews. Its logical underpinnings can be demolished in a handful of paragraphs:

First, relativism's friendship with tolerance is a masquerade. Relativism is, in actuality, the enemy of tolerance because it excuses intolerance. If the relativist cannot judge that one culture is really better than another, then, when he encounters a bigoted culture, he cannot judge that it behaves badly. Relativism, therefore, is as much a ratio-nale for intolerance as it is for tolerance. Relativists are clearly con-fused: On the one hand, they want to promote tolerance as an absolute value; on the other, they cannot promote it, because they do not be-lieve in absolutes.

One reason why relativism has cast its spell on culture today is that relativists have persuaded many people that relativism is necessary for a multicultural sensibility. But relativism undermines multiculturalism just as it defeats tolerance.[5] Relativism prohibits someone from con-demning another society's moral beliefs and practices, but it also pro-hibits someone from praising another society. If judgments are forbidden, praise is eliminated as surely as condemnation. This fact embarrasses the relativist. Instead of inspiring inclusiveness, relativism entails *isolationism*. Pushed to its logical conclusion, relativism must be mute (whether in praise or criticism) of other cultures.

Relativism makes the idea of progress impossible. Relativism pos-tures as progressive, but it cannot be so. If no defensible moral standards exist, we have no way to judge that one society is more advanced than another. But progress depends on our ability to make that determina-tion. For example, the United States of America has progressed because it has abolished slavery. The society America is today approximates better (at least on the slavery issue) the philosophical standard of free-dom than did American society in, say, 1850. American society in the first half of the nineteenth century fell miserably short of that standard. Reasonable people everywhere concur. The relativist, however, cannot belong to that company of reasonable people. For, according to relativ-ism, no such standards of better or worse exist. As relativists do not believe in rationally justifiable moral norms, they cannot argue that America has really improved, only that America has changed.

To take another example: Relativists delight in saying that Catholics have "progressed" because they no longer burn heretics, censure scien-tists, or condemn secular government rather than theocracy. Relativists might intend to compliment Catholics, but they cannot (if they remain consistent) praise Catholic culture, or any other, as progressive. Prog-ress presupposes standards (such as religious autonomy, free scientific inquiry, and separation of Church and State) for improvement, and

---

[5] In an excellent essay, Mary Midgley shows why relativism cannot celebrate cultural diversity: "Trying Out One's New Sword," *Heart and Mind: Varieties of Moral Experience* (New York: St. Martin's Press, 1981).

some societies incorporate those standards better than others. If relativists deny that such standards exist, they cannot assert that, in the past, Catholicism failed to meet those standards but that now it attains them. However, Catholics and others who believe that moral norms exist can justify and applaud progress. Therefore, Catholics, not relativists, can rightly and proudly call themselves "progressive" (however much sometimes they might have fallen short of that standard in the past).

Relativism promotes no tolerance, pluralism, or progress, while the Catholicism it condemns as intolerant champions each. Here we taste another irony, one that is no mere morsel. For the Catholic educator, part of a Catholic teacher's calling is to help students appreciate the philosophically defensible moral and social teachings *for all people* that radiate out of the Church and the gospel. Catholic education is essential in today's world because, by guarding against the insidious influences of relativism, it can rehabilitate a society crippled by relativism.

Question 2. Catholicism is an anachronism in a scientific age, that is, in an age dominated by physical science. Darwinian science has shown that human beings, like everything else in the universe, are products of physics. J. Baird Callicott has summarized this paradigm: "From the point of view of evolutionary theory as it has been extended in twentieth-century science, there is a historical continuity of human with animal life, and of animal life with plant life, and of life *in toto* with non-living chemical compounds, and so on right down to the most elementary physical constituents of nature."[6]

Because almost two centuries of physical and biological science have corroborated this paradigm, Catholic educators are irresponsible and unscientific in teaching a worldview that is incompatible with Darwinian reductionism. All that exists is matter in its various forms, including all life. In this worldview (alternatively called "naturalism"), we inhabit a Godless, purposeless universe. Human beings are not special creations of a loving God. We do not have immaterial, immortal souls. No "Day of Judgment" awaits us. *Does not the vindication by modern physical and biological science of the naturalist's worldview cancel out as unenlightened the Catholic worldview?*

Response. This question and objection make explicit a common presumption among today's intelligentsia, that *philosophical naturalism*

[6] J. Baird Callicott, "The Search for an Environmental Ethic," *Matters of Life and Death,* ed. Tom Regan (2d ed., New York: Random House, 1986), p. 387.

ought to prevail. Catholic elementary educators will find naturalism underlying many educational theories. To help in detecting this influence and in judging its importance, a few distinctions are in order.

(a) "Philosophical naturalism" is not the same as "methodological naturalism." The second simply refers to the fact that, by definition, physical science uses the habits of physical scientific method—observation, experiment, and measurement—to justify its claims to knowledge. Methodological naturalism is a way of saying that physical science searches for physical, not *trans*physical or *supernatural*, causes in explaining physical phenomena.

(b) Philosophical naturalism, on the other hand, is a *metaphysical*, not a physical scientific, claim. Metaphysics is a philosophical attempt to describe reality comprehensively. For example, Catholic metaphysics states that reality consists of both physical or natural things and non-physical realities, such as God, angels, and human souls. Philosophical naturalism denies that non-physical things exist. It reduces reality to physical things; it says only matter in motion exists. For this reason, it is sometimes called "physical reductionism." For philosophical naturalism, metaphysics is nothing more than physics.

(c) Methodological naturalism is perfectly congenial with Catholicism. Physical science is a method of discovery and explanation in God's physical creation. Philosophical naturalism, on the other hand, is not compatible with Catholicism because philosophical naturalism is atheism. Philosophical naturalism denies God's existence, God's special creation of human persons, and the immateriality and immortality of human souls. Take these away, and nothing is left of Catholicism.

Catholic educators must clearly be vigilant about philosophical naturalism insinuating itself into Catholic schools. This insinuation sometimes happens in routine instruction in the physical sciences, especially in some physical science textbooks. This happens when educators naïvely assume that advances in physical science demonstrate that philosophical naturalism is true. In the wider educated culture, prominent apologists for philosophical naturalism, such as Carl Sagan, Richard Dawkins, Stephen Hawking, and Stephen Jay Gould, have exploited with persuasive effect that naïve and false assumption.

A second set of distinctions has to do with evolution. Catholic teachers must be on guard about use of the word *evolution* inside or outside the classroom. We use the word in three different senses. Only one of them is incompatible with Catholic philosophy.

(a) "Evolution" sometimes refers merely to the fossil record—the geological evidence that natural history reflects stages from the non-living to the living, and from simple forms of life to complex forms, culminating in the latest geological era in which the species *homo sapiens* dominates the planet.

(b) "Evolution" may refer to the *mechanisms* of natural selection, mutation, and genetics that supposedly account for adaptations and changes of species recorded in the fossil record.

(c) "Evolution" may assert that the universe is a Godless, purpose-less system of matter in motion; that life in general and human life in particular resulted from accidents of nature, not from special creation of a providential God. In this third usage, "evolution" is equivalent to atheism or philosophical naturalism.

Evolution (a) or (b) is compatible with Catholic philosophy. God could have designed natural history to take whatever course He wanted. That living things appeared after aeons of non-living things, that complex forms were subsequent to simpler forms, that human beings appeared after hundreds of millions of years of other life-forms, are events logically consistent with the power and plan of a providential God. Furthermore, God could have used whatever mechanisms He wanted to develop natural history.

A Catholic philosopher must reject usage (c). Evolution as a camou-flage for atheism or philosophical naturalism is inimical to Catholic education. Catholic elementary teachers must have their philosophical antennas ready to detect its approach.

In sum, we answer by saying that physical science does not neces-sarily vindicate philosophical naturalism, because the scope and meth-ods of physical science are perfectly compatible with a worldview that includes supernatural things and other ways of knowing besides physical science. Equipped with the above distinctions, a Catholic teacher can defend the Catholic worldview against those who call it "unenlightened."

Question 3. The philosophers Jean-Jacques Rousseau (1712–1778) and John Dewey (1859–1952) have profoundly influenced modern educa-tion, especially the movement called "progressive education," and for good reason. They understood that effective learning is ultimately self-learning. Education, then, must inspire the child to want to develop his abilities and to commit to social involvement. This is education in the spirit of democracy. One hundred years before popes in their encyclicals were fumbling to praise democracy faintly, Rousseau was changing Europe with his democratic philosophy. *Are not thinkers like Rousseau and Dewey better guides for education in a democratic society than voices in the Catholic tradition with its coercive, even oppressive, and anti-democratic history?*

Response. To address this question, let us first briefly summarize Rousseau's and Dewey's views on education.

It is difficult to overstate the influence of Rousseau on modern culture. Politics and education over the last two centuries echo Rousseau's philosophy. His views on education radiate largely from his novel *Émile*. He believed that unenlightened civilization corrupts. Enlightened, or progressive, education, then, must be a program to avoid corruption. Unenlightened society and its teachers must keep their "hands off" the student.

Rousseau believed in the innate perfectibility of human beings. Minimizing social interference will reduce the risk of corruptions. Hence, education should let nature take its course. The child should live in a way uninhibited by unenlightened minds. A child needs to be totally self-habituated or habituated through contact only with "enlightened" minds. Enlightened teachers are exceptions to a meddlesome culture. They properly understand their role as facilitators. They do not impose content or programs on a child's mind. The child's own nature contains the voice of enlightened conscience and pure reason. By listening to his innate conscience and reason, each child will develop with sureness. Hence, permissiveness is a necessary condition for intellectual and moral growth.

Rousseau was confident that by developing an awareness of pity, sympathy, and a variety of other human sentiments, the educated youth will transcend his selfish nature and discover the worth of others. Eventually, this process will reveal the goal of enlightened education: an awareness of humanity and a solidarity with it. This goal can be reached if education allows the freedom for the child and young adult to develop his *natural* tendencies. Systems of education that impose classical curricula and morality stymie this development. Christian education is especially pernicious because it denies man's innate perfectibility through its doctrine of original sin. Without religion and religious schools, human beings will unfold from within their natural tendencies, which, if left unimpeded by the corruptions and interferences of "civilization," will impel human beings to construct an "enlightened" society of humanity, a utopian order of "heaven on earth." True education serves this purpose.

The context for John Dewey's influence is this: Over the past millennium, as philosophy mutated into logic and rhetoric, there was a change in the way modern philosophers use logic and language to associate their craft with physical science. By employing logic and quasi-scientific language, they imitate physical science, which enjoys esteem in modern society because of its practical and technological achievements. Hence, among modern thinkers, a temptation exists for philosophy to ape the physical sciences. In its extreme form, this imitation reduces philosophy to an "adjunct" of physical science. Philosophy becomes a tool for scientists to clarify their problems, hypotheses, theories, and methods. Dewey does not represent such an extreme, but he certainly thought that physical science provides the model for sound philosophy. Moreover, because he combined his regard for science with a philosophical naturalism, he constructed a view of philosophy in general, and a philosophy of education in particular, that is not, on the whole, agreeable to a Catholic philosophy of education.

Dewey's thought was part of a movement known as "pragmatism," which, like some other naturalistic philosophies, was partly inspired by Darwinism. Just as what is fit and suitable is what survives the trials of natural selection, so too, in the realm of ideas, what is true and valuable is what produces the most practical ("pragmatic") results. "A statement or an hypothesis is true or false insofar as it leads us to or away from the end which we have in view."[7] Dewey believed that pragmatism at its best should seek to imitate the laboratory techniques of physical science. "In practical experience, thought is an *instrument* in helping a person to adjust himself to the new in experience."[8] Truth is what works. Ideas are nothing more than instruments and plans of action for the self to better itself. Accordingly, Dewey's version of pragmatism he called "instrumentalism." When enlightened minds agree on what works, we have a social commitment to truth. Charles Sanders Peirce defined truth as "the limit towards which endless investigation would

[7] Frederick Copleston, *A History of Philosophy*, vol. 8, part 2 (Garden City, N.Y.: Image Books, 1967), p. 123.
[8] Harold A. Buetow, *The Catholic School: Its Roots, Identity, and Future* (New York: Crossroad Publishing Co., 1988), p. 29.

tend to bring scientific belief."[9] Truth, then, is social consensus about what does or does not work.

Dewey claimed that people's interpretations of reality are motivated solely by considerations of utility for themselves.[10] Education must build on this truth about human life: Human beings are motivated to do what is relevant and useful. Once educators create systems that inspire young people to discover that it is relevant and useful to produce a moral and social order good for humanity, education will at last have instrumental value as a "school for tomorrow," in service of democracy—hence the titles of two of Dewey's more important books, *Schools of Tomorrow* (1915) and *Democracy and Education* (1916). These titles make sense because people can see that a democratic society is best for them because it gives them the opportunities to better themselves. "His main conviction is that education should not be simply instruction in various subjects but rather a coherent unified effort to foster the development of citizens capable of promoting the further growth of society by employing intelligence fruitfully in a social context."[11]

Dewey doubted that schools, especially religious schools, that are built on classical curricula have the instrumental vitality to educate for democratic ends. Hence, education needs reform so as to institute "experimental" schools. Such schools will enable students, somewhat in the spirit of Rousseau's educational vision, to discover their own natural tendencies. These tendencies will guide them in the formation of habits whereby they simultaneously discover that, by living and working for others, they help themselves. This is democracy's pragmatic, instrumental, experimental genius. The school must be a tool in its service. Dewey's philosophical naturalism and instrumentalism are the prescription for such a school.

While Dewey was suspicious of traditional religion, he substituted for it a religion of his own. Like Rousseau, Dewey deified "Humanity." His philosophical naturalism denied that supernatural beings, such as God and the human soul, exist. Nonetheless, he posited an object worthy of worship. It is a projection of the hopes, potentialities, and ideals of human life. In *A Common Faith* (1934), he defined being religious as faith "in the unification of the self through allegiance to

---

[9] Quoted in Dewey, *Logic: The Theory of Inquiry* (New York, 1938), p. 345, note 6.
[10] Buetow, *The Catholic School*, p. 29.
[11] Copleston, *A History of Philosophy*, vol. 8, part 2, p. 132.

inclusive ideal ends, which imagination presents to us and to which the human will responds as worthy of controlling our desires and choices." [12] If religion means an object of "ultimate concern," Dewey is a religious man, even if his religion is unlike Catholic faith in a supernatural, providential, Creator God. Dewey's ultimate concern is the effort to attain goals that ensure the flourishing of human freedom and social development. This is the ideal of democracy that perpetuates the ideal of "Humanity." The school is an instrument for these ideals. This is the only "religious school" that Dewey can justify.

Obviously, we can appreciate the effort by Rousseau and Dewey to recover a sense of relevance and practicality in the classroom. The reminder that education must cooperate with the natural tendencies of children is a tonic for dull instruction. Pragmatism reminds us that our intelligence involves physical action. We sense with our intellects; we intellectualize with our senses. Our intelligence involves choice, and choice is never about things; it always involves action. Moreover, as a method for problem-solving, pragmatism has value. It appreciates the physical and practical in human experience.

As for Rousseau, an enlightened society for humanity does emerge as conscience instructs us to regard others' feelings as equal to our own. This sentiment is the basis of duty, justice, and love. In Rousseau's utopia, free expression guarantees harmony. It follows that religious freedom must exist. But Rousseau's hostility to Catholicism is evident, as Peter A. Redpath notes:

> According to Rousseau, duty requires religious tolerance. From a practical, everyday standpoint, this means that duty requires us to accept the Westphalian notion of following the religion of our country, with one major exception. Since Rousseau defines conscience as the voice of love of the human good, and since he defines the human good as the love of humanity (which love, he thinks, is the same as justice), by definition, for him, the "love of the religion of one's country does not extend to dogmas contrary to good morals."
>
> Such dogmas, however, include those which claim that the love of humanity is not the highest moral good, as, for instance, any believing Jew, Christian, or Muslim would hold. In Rousseau's

---

[12] Ibid., p. 133.

view, such religious notions are hostile to good morals, intolerant and intolerable.[13]

With such a double standard for tolerance, Rousseau's program does not tolerate Catholic education. Here is an instance of a double standard still prevalent among many of Rousseau's intellectual descendants. In Rousseau is the prejudgment that Catholicism is the enemy of freedom, of human nature, and of a human society. Instead of naïvely and uncritically accepting Rousseau's influence, the Catholic educator guards against it and puts it on the defensive, by showing how the Catholic worldview powerfully defends and advocates true freedom, humanity, and justice in society. In today's cultural climate, Catholic teachers must be prepared to do so over protests of Rousseau's descendants, today's children of toleration. For Étienne Gilson's judgment still rings true: "Anti-Catholicism is the anti-Semitism of the [Rousseauian] intellectuals."

In addition, we can direct several criticisms at Dewey's philosophy of education.

(a) Dewey's instrumentalism mistakes verification for truth. The practical effects of a belief and its ability to win social consensus might be signs of truth, but we ought not confuse them with truth. Truth is the intellect's conformity to the way things actually are, which may have nothing to do with practicality or consensus.

(b) Dewey's allegiance to philosophical naturalism inclines him to give the last word to what is physically observable, measurable, and experimental. This attitude, however, is limited in ways Dewey himself might not have appreciated. While all knowledge starts in sense experience, our intellects can infer that objects exist that transcend the range of sense knowledge, such as God, human souls, and morality. Dewey's philosophical naturalism by definition rules out these objects; for a philosophical naturalist, only matter exists. But naturalists are self-refuting in that they reduce knowledge to observation, measurement, or experimentation. For the idea that "knowledge is only what is observed, measured, or experimented upon" is not verifiable by the standards of observation, measurement, and experimentation.

(c) Dewey's pragmatism is limited as a theory of morality. Social consensus has rationalized every kind of injustice in history, from

[13] Peter A. Redpath, *Masquerade of the Dream Walkers: Prophetic Theology from the Cartesians to Hegel* (Amsterdam, The Netherlands: Editions Rodopi B.V., 1998), p. 96.

slavery to denial of women's suffrage. Therefore, we have another reason to suspect that a theory that declares "truth is what works" does not work. "Truth for the pragmatist is sociologically certified agreement. This admits of the equation of prevalence with normalcy—hardly an acceptable criterion for Catholic morality."[14]

A philosophy that emphasizes *relevance* runs the risk of this kind of error. Consensus makes ideas relevant by creating cultural support for them, or even a "social buzz" around them. But as Harold Buetow has observed: "Although it is true that the thinker should concern himself with what is relevant, one should speculate about all aspects of being. That which is important has an inner weight of its own, even when not perceived as relevant. What many people have perceived as being relevant here and now has often in the long run turned out to be unimportant."[15]

(d) One can agree that a teacher is a "facilitator," but a Catholic philosophy of elementary education understands "facilitator" differently from the way Dewey used the word. A Catholic teacher is an informed and interactive facilitator—interactive because she engages the child in conversation and has something authoritative, directive, and substantive to offer. She facilitates the discovery and exploration of content and is not merely a facilitator who keeps order in the classroom—a room of students free to move from subject to subject by whim or impulse. To Dewey's credit, he recognized eventually that a laissez-faire classroom was unrealistic.

> There is a present tendency in so-called advanced schools of thought . . . to say, in effect, let us surround pupils with certain materials, tools, appliances, etc., and then let pupils respond to these things according to their own desires. Above all, let us not suggest any end or plan to the students; let us not suggest to them what they shall do, for that is an unwarranted trespass upon their sacred intellectual individuality. . . . Now such a method is really stupid. For it attempts the impossible, which is always stupid; and it misconceives the conditions of independent thinking.[16]

[14] Buetow, *The Catholic School*, p. 30.
[15] Ibid.
[16] Diane Ravitch, *Left Back: A Century of Battles over School Reform*, p. 199.

With these critical words, Dewey's view of the classroom conforms to a description that the Catholic educator can accept. Still, the Deweyan model of child development brings the risk that the teacher become too passive and that classrooms become anarchical. One could imagine a devotee of Dewey's instrumentalism arguing with the master that he is truer to the free spirit of Dewey's pedagogy than the master himself and might stand by this thesis even though the latter calls such methods "stupid."

(e) Dewey, like Rousseau, believed that religion has its source in human desires and projections, in self-revelation, not in divine revelation. Clearly, such an attitude contradicts the substance of Catholic schooling. Revelation makes no sense according to philosophical naturalism, and therefore is an idea forbidden by this educational philosophy.

(f) According to Dewey, religion has value only when it is practical for the individual and beneficial to society. The value of religion—which ideally is humanistic—is that it gives solidarity and optimism to the human race. So, to judge the value of religion is to judge its excitement in society at a given moment in history. This view of religion is at odds with Catholicism, for Catholics see religion as having objective worth whether or not it pleases a specific individual or a specific society at any given time.[17]

(g) A catch-phrase out of the Deweyan era in education is that schooling should be "child-centered." But as Father Buetow points out, however much Catholic education must love children, Catholic education is God-centered, not child-centered.[18] Besides, how can education really be "child-centered," if it ignores a child's spiritual nature and ultimate destiny? Furthermore, for a Catholic, a child-centered education must teach morality, but natural law and virtue-ethics are beyond the reach of Dewey's empiricism. Thus, a Catholic education in moral habits involves far more than Dewey's philosophical naturalism could allow.

The influence of Rousseau and Dewey have derailed education—from perfecting a human person's faculties, to producing a project for social progressivism. Authentic Catholic education collides with a

---

[17] Buetow, *The Catholic School*, p. 30. A disturbing recent summation of how anti-Catholicism remains an "acceptable prejudice" in American society is Philip Jenkins' *The New Anti-Catholicism* (New York: Oxford Press, 2003).

[18] Buetow, *The Catholic School*, pp. 30–31.

Rousseau-Deweyan model of education. The latter turns the school into a social-work program that produces untrained minds receptive to direction by propaganda. The school instead should be primarily about intellectual formation, putting the student into contact with the truth of things. A philosophy that adequately explains the truths of things must involve far more than instrumentalism and social agendas. Catholic theology, metaphysics, morality, and philosophy of the human person provide a more comprehensive context for explaining the truth of things.

Question 4. Education's task is to deepen students' appreciation of questions. Human beings cannot with assurance give conclusive answers. To be more aware that human beings are question-asking animals is the proper aim of schooling. Life and the universe are mysteries. To Pilate's question "What is Truth?" Jesus gave no philosophical reply. *Are not Catholic educators vain and arrogant in their presumption that they know the truth and that they can teach the truth to others?*

Response. Today, many have become very ambivalent about the word "truth." On the one hand, we still make statements that we insist are true. We also call "liars" those who say something is true when they know it is not. Use of and reference to the "truth" is as common today as it has ever been. On the other hand, if you use the word "truth" in a general sense—as in statements like "I know the truth"; "the value of education consists in teaching the truth"; "culture decays if people no longer believe in the truth"—you would likely be met with quizzical looks. You are likely to be told that a "true" educator knows that nobody can say what is really true. It is "arrogant" and probably dangerous in present-day culture to teach students on the presumption that you know the truth. Hence, enlightened minds do not admit to knowing the truth, a popular sentiment Howard Gardner states this way:

> On my educational landscape, questions are more important than answers; knowledge and, more important, understanding should evolve from the constant probing of such questions. It's not because I know for certain what the true and the beautiful and the good are that I call for their study. In fact, I distrust people who claim that they *know* what is true, beautiful, or good. I organize my presentation around these topics because they motivate individuals to learn about and understand their world, and because,

frankly, I reject a world in which individuals cease to pursue these essential questions just because they do not permit unequivocal resolution.[19]

Gardner offers a sincere statement. But he is unaware that it is self-contradictory. First, if his "educational landscape" produced excellent and informed human beings, would they not, by his own standards, be good and beautiful? Would not such excellence be a *true* standard for education? Second, Gardner is sure and judgmental in distrusting people who believe in truth, goodness and beauty (in other words, people who disagree with him). Third, his closing remark is a judgment that skepticism is preferable to nonskepticism. But this is another truth-claim: "It is true that for educators skepticism is better than nonskepticism." So, again, he contradicts himself. Why does he get to make truth-claims, while others do not?

This is just another example of how relativism confuses people into saying something incoherent. As we have discussed, relativism about morals and truth is quite common in today's academy. Educators, especially educational "theorists," often respond (predictably) as skeptics about truth.

But Catholics cannot afford to be confused about truth's nature. So, some further remarks are in order.

(a) We may ask with Pilate, "What is truth?" But as everyone uses the word *truth* daily, it cannot be as mysterious as Pilate makes it appear. If you are involved in a traffic accident and the investigating policeman asks, "Did you run the red light?" it would be no mystery to the forty witnesses to the accident what you should say to answer the question truthfully. If you answer falsely, forty people will know that you have lied. This seemingly trivial example makes the point that the truth is evident in common-sense experience. No one needs to be trained in academic philosophy to differentiate between truth-tellers and liars. When we make judgments that agree with the facts, we report the truth. So, we *can* reply to Pilate's question: Truth is a judgment that agrees with reality.

(b) However, usually when people ask Pilate's question, they nuance it in ways that make a simple and direct answer insufficient. Often, reasonable people will disagree about what is true. In fact,

---

[19] Howard Gardner, *The Disciplined Mind* (London: Penguin Books, 2000), p. 24.

Pilate's question is an inexact version of one of two other questions that the Pilate-like inquirer really has in mind: (1) "Is there ultimate or absolute Truth?" or (2) "When subjects are difficult or controversial, can the human knower determine the truth?" (This latter question is especially troublesome, given that evidence is often partial and conflicting.) Responding to these alternative formulations is worthwhile because some important issues in Catholicism and in Catholic education are brought to light.

The question *Is there ultimate or absolute Truth?* is asking whether a perfect being exists. If truth is agreement with what actually is, then that which is *most true* will express what is most actual. Accordingly, Absolute Truth is Absolute Being. In Catholic teaching, "God" is the answer to this question. In the Gospel of John, Jesus was silent before Pilate's question. If Jesus is God, He Himself is the answer to Pilate's question. Pilate is staring at the answer to his question. Ultimate or Absolute Truth is a "Who," the Person of Jesus Christ, not a "What." Jesus remained silent because there is no point in proving the obvious.

As for the second version, *Can we determine truth, inasmuch as judgments of truth often conflict and are controversial?* countless distinctions might be in order. There are two general aspects we might consider here. Broadly speaking, the question arises because of plural evidences, or lack thereof, on the side of *the object* (the thing people dispute), or because of interpretations on the side of *the subject* (the people who disagree).

For example, controversy over whether there is life on other planets. Not enough evidence exists on either side of the disagreement to resolve it. Another example: Is traditional ("Western") or alternative ("holistic" or "Eastern") medicine better for the treatment of certain ailments? Here disagreement exists because both parties in the dispute can make persuasive cases, because each has evidence to show. It does not follow from their disagreement that no truths exist.

The Dred Scott decision is another case we could cite in illustration. The Justices on the U.S. Supreme Court, in 1856, found something controversial that ought not to be controversial. Escaping their prejudices, we would expect no reasonable person today to reach a decision that African-Americans are only three-fifths persons. This case discloses something important: a possible reason for disagreement about the truth is that some people are intellectually limited (by, for example, ignorance or prejudice) and thus unable to adjudicate the disagreement. Those who escape such limitations simply see a solution or judge the truth more clearly. But their judgment might not be accepted because ignorance, prejudice, or stupidity might cloud the judgment of the other parties in the dispute. That possibility has to be eliminated before we have the right to argue a wholesale skepticism or relativism about truth.

In light of these comments, Catholic philosophy can assure us that judgments of truth are possible, even when they are controversial. Moreover, reason and Revelation show that Absolute Truth exists.

Question 5. Catholic moral philosophers belabor virtue-ethics and natural law. This is not necessary, for psychological theories of cognitive moral development exist, such as the theory proposed by Lawrence Kohlberg, that are quite as convincing. Kohlberg can be as reliable a guide for a teacher aiming to understand the moral development of children as Aristotle or Aquinas. *Can we not substitute a modern, simple theory like Lawrence Kohlberg's "stages of moral development" for the virtue-ethics tradition in Catholic elementary schooling?*

Response. Kohlberg's model takes ethics to be a system that supplies rules whose skillful use enables a person to solve moral problems. Ethics is a way of *logically* working through moral difficulties. In the early stages of life, a boy or girl has only a very primitive and implicit "rule" or "system." Such "rules" as "pursue pleasure and avoid pain" or "please Mommy and Daddy" or "please yourself" may be all that constitute the "moral system" of childhood. But as the child matures, his logical skills should develop. A child's ability to reason about morality becomes more subtle. Soon, the standard for correct logical thinking in morality becomes *social* authority: teachers, parents, and, most important, peers. An even more sophisticated development is reliance on civil laws as the moral standard (that is, what is moral is what is legal). To stop moral development at this stage, however, would stunt a person's cognitive moral growth. Once a person is an adult, he should be able to start articulating moral justifications in logical and systematic terms. Hence, we expect developing moral minds to learn eventually to use principles suggestive of *social contract* (I promise not to hurt you if you don't hurt me) or *utility* (my action is permissible if it helps others or, at least, if it doesn't harm others). The zenith of moral development comes when someone shows logical facility in relying on abstract, universal principles to solve moral difficulties. Examples of abstract moral principles are justice, rights, autonomy, and obligation. A mind that can nimbly use such principles to clarify and solve moral problems has attained Kohlberg's highest standard of cognitive moral development. In other words, a philosopher like Immanuel Kant (1724–1804), who tried to build an ethics exclusively around logic and rational rules, is Kohlberg's standard for the highest philosophical moral development.

For Catholic philosophy, the virtue-integration of the human person is the standard for morality. For Kohlberg, the standard of morality is logic. For Catholic moral philosophy, the development of habits makes a human life excellent. Moral virtue, not logic, is morality's center. For a Catholic moral philosophy, it is crucial to understand what it is to be a human being. Morality has to do with choices that are means toward the end of fulfilling our human nature. Morality is about moral virtue, not about parsing or abstracting logical moral principles. To reduce ethics to logic is to leave out of ethics its most important element: real relationships between flesh-and-blood human beings. Abstract principles might make moral problem-solving "simpler," but by *abstracting* (withdrawing) from the actual living context of human relations and by reducing human agents and their relations to a logical puzzle or game, abstractions cannot supply a complete ethics.

In Kohlberg's effort to explain ethics as manipulating abstract terms and principles, he renders ethics anemic and unsatisfactory. Ethics must engage human beings in their actual, living, historical and social context. It does violence to moral situations and relationships to reduce them to abstractions. This is a criticism made effectively by Kohlberg's protégé Carol Gilligan in her book *In A Different Voice*. She indicates that a sound ethics refuses to abstract from moral context in which human beings live and make decisions. Kohlberg fails because he does not understand virtue-ethics. Moral virtue takes into account justice and charity as habits in personal and social contexts. Because justice and charity are ways in which actual, living human beings order their social experience, an intelligent ethics will resist reducing moral problem-solving to conceptual analysis. In this light, Kohlberg's theory of cognitive development does not conform to a Catholic moral philosophy, where human nature, relationships, virtues (especially justice and charity), and actions-in-social-context take priority over conceptual analysis. Catholic ethics is "less tidy," but more human, than Kohlberg's program.

Catholics certainly believe in rules, commands and principles, but not as logical abstractions. Principles are worthwhile if they are historically based and have experiential causes. Each generation must apply and test them in its own distinctive way in the living laboratory of human social experience. For example, the Ten Commandments are reliable commands for human life, not because they are logical constructs, but because the record of human *experience* shows that it is impossible to live well individually and socially without them. Causal experience, not abstract logic, is our chief moral teacher.[20]

Question 6. Howard Gardner has criticized classical education as being narrow and simplistic in its definition of intelligence. Instead of having only one intelligence, as Greek and Catholic philosophers taught, we humans have multiple intelligences. *Can a Catholic philosophy of elementary education accommodate the idea of multiple intelligences?*

Response. Often, disagreements arise because of the way we describe our theories. Intelligence involves a diversity of activities that can come under the control of habits or skills. If we want to call these different ways of knowing and acting "multiple intelligences," we should speak more precisely when we talk of one faculty of intellect operating in different ways than when we speak of many intellects. Then, again, we may excuse Gardner's idea of "multiple intelligences" as a way of emphasizing the diverse abilities of intellect.

> Intelligence tests typically tap linguistic and logical-mathematical intelligence—the intelligences of greatest moment in contemporary schools—perhaps sampling spatial intelligence as well. But as a species we also possess musical intelligence, bodily-kinesthetic intelligence, naturalistic intelligence, intelligence about ourselves (intra-personal intelligence), and intelligence about other persons (inter-personal intelligence). And it is possible that human beings also exhibit a ninth, existential intelligence—the proclivity to pose (and ponder) questions about life, death, and ultimate realities.[21]

[20] For a summary of Kohlberg's work that also contains a reply to Gilligan, see *The Psychology of Moral Development*, vols 1 and 2 (New York: Harper & Row, 1984); see also Carol Gilligan, *In a Different Voice: Psychological Theory and Women's Development* (Harvard University Press, 1982).

[21] Gardner, *The Disciplined Mind*, p. 72.

Different children have different capacities in the way they exercise their intellects, and Gardner's idea of multiple intelligences is his way of endorsing individualized or "differentiated" education. Not all students are the same. So teachers and curricula must be able to develop each child individually.

I find nothing incompatible with a Catholic philosophy of elementary education in Gardner's remarks provided we recognize only *one* faculty of intellect that has *many abilities and habits.* By stressing diverse uses of the intellect, Gardner, in his own way, reiterates Gilson's key insight about the human being as an embodied knower: We sense with our intelligence, and we intellectualize with our senses. A Catholic philosophy appreciates that the acts of the intellect—concept, judgment and reasoning—involve actions with our physical nature. Our intellect interacts with our internal and external senses as our bodies engage the physical world. Abstraction, judgment, and reasoning are constantly at work as our senses respond to things in multiple ways. To Gardner's credit, he is sensitive to this fact. He reminds us that we must be on guard against a view of intelligence as purely linguistic and logical, as though intelligence were disembodied. Disembodied intelligence is the intelligence of angels, not of school children. Accordingly, we can agree with Gardner's "critique of the notion of a single intelligence, and of a school curriculum targeted exclusively to linguistic and logical capacities and concerns." [22]

Question 7. Social scientific research about the nature and causes of learning has passed by Catholic philosophy of elementary education. Social science has accumulated convincing evidence that knowledge is social. We learn through the influences of our social and individual history. Acquisition of knowledge is a sociological phenomenon, a conclusion expressed in a social scientific theory of learning called "Social Construct Theory." Does not such a theory show that knowledge is relativized? *If social structures determine knowledge, then will not knowledge of similar subjects differ significantly in individuals living in different cultures? Is not this powerful scientific evidence against the Catholic philosopher's criticism of relativism?*

Response. Another way that relativism percolates in the academy is through the fashion of "social construct theory." Like so many fads

[22] Ibid., p. 25.

and trends, social construct theory takes a grain of truth and extrapolates from it a mountain of fallacies. The grain of truth is that our culture, place, and time in history, and our immediate environment influence our learning. This is obvious, an observation nobody ever disputed. Who denies that we "bring baggage" to our learning experiences? But social-construct theorists go much farther, insisting that politics and culture *produce* structures in our minds by which we *construct* experience. The word "construct" implies an anti-realist, skeptical view of knowledge. Structures inside the mind, not experience of things outside the mind, supposedly determine the content of our knowledge.

This anti-realism is implicit in the name for the theory, "social *construct* theory." It is not called "social *influence* theory," a moderate position that a realist could perhaps accommodate. Social-construct theory substitutes anti-realism for realism, thereby gravitating toward the extreme and incredible position that human knowledge is merely a construction through the "constructs" of culture, tradition, social, and personal background.

This bizarre view has become mainstream in certain segments of educational culture. Virtually an educational industry has become associated with social construct theory, especially among some multiculturalists who insist that race, gender, and politics determine learning.[23] This theory often involves amusing twists and turns. For example, in conversation with social construct theorists, one hears them sometimes complain about grade inflation, social promotion, and erosion of academic standards in general.[24]

A simple distinction exposes the social construct theory as fallacious and counter-intuitive. We must distinguish learning's *process* from its *object; how* we come to know from *what* we know. As noted earlier, nobody denies that all kinds of influences affect learning; such influences undoubtedly include race, gender, and politics. Perhaps the

[23] I regularly receive catalogues from prominent university presses distinguishing "Colonial" and "Post-Colonial" science from "North-Atlantic Science." They also refer to books whose themes warn against eurocentrism, logocentrism, androcentrism, and many other "centrisms." They advance books committed to social construct theory, which promotes relativism and politics in its account of learning.

[24] One social construct theorist I know is on a crusade to restore rigor to our classrooms. I have to smile when I hear his complaints. For, according to his own theory of knowledge, standards for evaluating students, like all acts of knowing, necessarily involve political and social constructions. Therefore, social construct theory is a tailor-made excuse for grading and promoting students for political reasons!

way Mrs. Abel taught me the multiplication table at John Adams Elementary School in Oklahoma City involved race, gender, and politics. Mrs. Abel was a Caucasian woman (race and gender), teaching a Caucasian boy (race and gender), in a public school in a conservative state (politics). But again, this is a trivial truth. No reasonable person ever denied that cultural factors somewhat condition how a child learns.

The question is: Beyond this *process* or conditioning, what bearing do these cultural elements have on the *content* of learning? The answer is clear: none. I may have learned the multiplication table under particular conditions and influences, but to assert that my multiplication is irreducibly "Oklahoman" would be absurd. Regardless of different personal backgrounds and "social constructions," multiplication is the same for everybody. I expect someone from West Virginia or Patagonia to calculate correctly, by the same standards. Everywhere in the Americas five times five is twenty-five. Through knowledge and judgment, the human intellect can transcend its circumstances and know timeless truths. Social construct theory, like all forms of relativism, denies the possibility of such transcendence.

So, we accept the grain of truth, but reject the mountain of fallacies. Still, it is surprising (and humorous) how social construct theory sways academicians. For example, a mathematics course taught in 1995 at the State University of New York–Plattsburgh, "Mathematics, Gender, and Culture," included the following objectives: (1) "describe the political nature of mathematics and mathematics education"; (2) "describe gender and race differences in mathematics and their sociological consequences"; (3) "examine the factors influencing gender and race differences in mathematics"; (4) "describe the role culture plays in the development and learning of mathematics"; (5) "describe the relationship of gender and culture to mathematics and mathematics education." [25]

Most of these objectives fail to distinguish the process of learning from the content learned. Only the fourth objective appears perfectly acceptable. The others are unacceptable or are only partly acceptable. For example, the first-named objective is partly intelligent, but it is absurd to imply that mathematics, as regards what it *knows*, is political. The square root of 16 has no race, gender, or party affiliation.

In my judgment, social construct theory is an especially pernicious

[25] Cited in *National Association of Scholars News List*, Seventh National Conference Edition (December 1997), p. 1.

fashion. It uses relativism to insinuate raw political power into educational policy, programs, and classrooms. Armed with the distinctions I outlined earlier, the Catholic elementary teacher can escape the snares and pitfalls of social construct theory.[26]

Question 8. Neurological science has significantly advanced in its knowledge of the brain. This knowledge of the brain will revolutionize education as teachers increasingly recognize that understanding brain function is necessary to teach students effectively. *Is not a Catholic philosophy of elementary education, with its archaic talk of faculty psychology, habits, and virtues, unscientific and unreceptive to what Howard Gardner has called "the Cognitive Revolution," the new science of the brain, in education? Does not this revolution mean that philosophical naturalism, as against Catholic philosophy, will have the last word in education?*

Response. The Catholic teacher must be cautious about "brain-talk" in the profession. It often camouflages a philosophical naturalism about the human person, the belief that human beings are only organic machines. Clearly, any such account of the human person is incompatible with a Catholic philosophy of human learning.

Certainly, brains matter. As embodied creatures, we depend on our bodies to engage our world and convey us information. Without our brains and central nervous system, experience could not take place. Our conscious life is necessarily dependent on these organs. But the dependency of our conscious lives on the brain does not mean that consciousness *is* the brain or is merely a by-product of brain processes. Neurological science has not shown that awarenesses is identical with brain states or events. It can establish only that brain actions *correlate* with mental states.

For example, when someone has a toothache, potassium chloride is secreted in his amygdyla. But to say that the pain *is* potassium chloride is an unwarranted inference. A gulf exists between the nature of conscious states and brain states. This is so, even if potassium chloride *causes* the pain; for the *awareness* of pain is not the same as the chemistry of pain. Chemicals and chemical actions have properties (such as mass, weight, location, velocity) that do not describe mental states. Neurology does not deny that gulf. Educators and philosophers,

---

[26] I present a detailed critique of social-construct theory in "Social Construct Theory: Relativism's Latest Fashion," in *The Failure of Modernism*, ed. Brendan Sweetman (Washington, D.C.: The Catholic University of America Press, 1999), pp. 242–258.

convinced by philosophical naturalism and the supposition that physical science can explain (or explain away) everything, sometimes claim that that gulf is an illusion. Neurologists, as a rule, are more cautious and not driven by naturalist ideology. Hence, they concede that neurological science might someday provide an exhaustive map of the brain but doubt that such a map will necessarily reveal what someone thinks or feels.

As a result, this so-called "cognitive revolution" regarding brain and education is of mixed value. A Catholic educator must appreciate that since we are embodied creatures, science of the brain is crucial for better understanding the human person and effectively giving new insights and directions for teaching. But because this "cognitive revolution" might mask a naturalist ideology (by identifying the human knower with brain states and processes), we must limit its influence on Catholic education. Like so many trends and theories, it is only partly acceptable. Part of the story of human life is that human beings are bodies. But because Catholic wisdom teaches that we are bodies-and-souls, a naturalist account of the human person would derail a Catholic elementary education.[27]

DISCUSSION QUESTIONS

1 "In the area of belief on the part of Catholic educators, what would you posit as minimum?" [28]

2. "To what extent should a child be encouraged to acquire self-direction over and against being dependent upon authority?"

3. "Do the psychological theories pertaining to the growth and development of the person address the idea of spirituality?"

4. "Can a school teach self-discipline? What is the purpose of discipline in a Catholic school?"

5. "How necessary is the personal presence of the teacher? Will technological improvements, such as computer-assisted instruction, do away with the need for the teacher? If the personal presence of the teacher is necessary, what consequences flow from that?"

[27] For a critical discussion of some current theories on brain theory and their philosophical implications, see Curtis Hancock and Brendan Sweetman, *Truth and Religious Belief* (Armonk, New York: M. E. Sharpe, 1998), chap. 4.

[28] Except for numbers 9 and 15, these questions appeared first in Harold A. Buetow, *The Catholic School.*

6. "If teaching and learning are correlative terms, is it necessary for true teaching that learning take place?"

7. "What is the source of the teacher's authority: subject-matter mastery, superiors, delegation from parents, participation in the parenthood of God, or what?"

8. "What about atheists being permitted to teach in Catholic schools? Non-Catholic Christians? Non-Christian religious?"

9. A friend sports the t-shirt "I survived Catholic school." People often express ambivalence (or worse) about their Catholic elementary schooling. What is the source of this attitude? Is it well founded?

10. "Given present-day realities, many 'enlightened' people say that young people are going to do it anyway, so rather than waste time shouting a futile, 'Don't,' maybe we ought only to teach them to do it responsibly. Supply them with the information, the resources, and the devices to eliminate the worst of the consequences of their doing it. Would the same 'enlightened' people maintain the same position with drugs as with sex? Why or why not?"

11. "Can a Catholic school truly create a climate that replicates that of the good Catholic home? If so, how?"

12. "Why does Rousseau's naturalism make impossible any qualitative excellence in education?"

13. "In secularistic and pluralistic societies, why should the Church have any rights in schooling?"

14. "Should Catholic schools, especially where a good number of students or teachers are non-Catholics, merely teach *about* religion?"

15. Rousseauian and Deweyan education, resting on philosophical naturalism, is a kind of "secular humanism." What evidence exists that it is taught in government schools?

16. "How does one deal with a Catholic-school student's personal preference for agnosticism or atheism?"

BIBLIOGRAPHY

Abbeduto, Leonard, editor. *Taking Sides: Clashing Views on Controversial Issues in Educational Psychology*. Second Edition. Guilford, Conn.: McGraw-Hill/Dushkin, 2002.

Adler, Mortimer. "Are There Absolute and Universal Principles?" In *Reforming Education: The Opening of the American Mind*. New York: Macmillan, 1988.

———. *Aristotle for Everybody*. New York: Macmillan, 1978.

———. *How to Read a Book*. London: Jarrolds Publishers, 1949.

———. *A Guidebook to Learning*. New York: Macmillan, 1986.

———. "Liberalism and Liberal Education, 1939." In *Reforming Education: The Opening of the American Mind*. New York: Macmillan, 1988.

Allen, Steve. *Dumbth: The Lost Art of Thinking*. New York: Prometheus Books, 1998.

Aquinas, Saint Thomas. *On the Teacher. Question Eleven of The Disputed Questions on Truth*. Translated by J. McGlynn. Vol. 2. Chicago: Henry Regnery Company, 1953.

Augustine, Saint. *The City of God*. Translated by Marcus Dods. In *Great Books of the Western World*. Vol. 18. Chicago: Encyclopedia Britannica, 1952.

———. *On the Teacher*. In *Augustine: Earlier Writings*. Edited by J. H. S. Burleigh. Philadelphia: The Westminster Press, 1953.

Azevedo, Milton M., and Kathryn K. McMahon, editors. *Lecturas Periodisticas*. Lexington, Mass.: D. C. Heath, 1983.

Bennett, William J., editor. *The Book of Virtues*. New York: Simon & Schuster, 2004.

Bloom, Allan. *The Closing of the American Mind: How Higher Education Has Failed Democracy and Impoverished the Souls of Today's Students*. New York: Simon & Schuster, 1987.

Bonnette, Dennis. *Origin of the Human Species*. Amsterdam, The Netherlands: Editions Rodopi, 2001.

Boydston, Jo Ann, editor. *Guide to the Works of John Dewey*. Carbondale, Ill.: Southern Illinois University Press, 1970.

Broudy, Harry S. *Building a Philosophy of Education*. New York: Prentice Hall, 1954.

Buetow, Harold A. *The Catholic School: Its Roots, Identity, and Future*. New

York: Crossroad Publishing Company, 1988.

——. *Of Singular Benefit: The Story of U.S. Catholic Education*. New York: Macmillan, 1970.

Burden, Paul R., and David M. Byrd. *Methods for Effective Teaching*. Second Edition. Boston: Allyn and Bacon, 1999.

Byrnes, James T. *John Paul II and Educating for Life*. New York: Peter Lang Publishing, 2002.

Cahn, Steven M., editor. *Classic and Contemporary Readings in the Philosophy of Education*. New York: McGraw-Hill, 1997.

Callicott, J. Baird. "The Search for an Environmental Ethic." In *Matters of Life and Death*. Edited by Tom Regan. Second Edition. New York: Random House, 1986.

Copleston, Frederick. *A History of Philosophy*. Vols. 1–9. Garden City, N.Y.: Image Books, 1962–1980.

Cremin, Lawrence A. *The Transformation of the School: Progressivism in American Education, 1876–1957*. New York: Alfred A. Knopf, 1964.

Cunningham, William F. *The Pivotal Problems of Education: An Introduction to the Christian Philosophy of Education*. New York: Macmillan, 1940.

Curtis, Sarah A. *Educating the Faithful: Religion, Schooling, and Society in Nineteenth-Century France*. DeKalb, Ill.: Northern Illinois University Press, 2000.

De Hovre, Franz. *Catholicism in Education*. New York: Benziger Brothers, 1934.

Derrick, Christopher. *Escape from Skepticism: Teaching As Though Truth Mattered*. San Francisco: Ignatius Press, 2002.

Dewey, John. *The Child and the Curriculum*. Chicago: University of Chicago Press, 1902.

——. *Democracy and Education*. New York: Macmillan Publishing Company, 1916.

——. *Experience and Education*. New York: Kappa Delta Pi, 1938; reprint: New York: Simon & Schuster, 1997.

——. *Logic: The Theory of Inquiry*. New York: Simon & Schuster, 1938.

——. *Moral Principles in Education*. Boston: Houghton-Mifflin Company, 1909; reprint: Acturus Books, 1975.

——. *Problems of Men*. New York: Philosophical Library, 1946.

——. "Religion and Our Schools." *Hibbert Journal* 6 (July, 1908): 796–809.

——. *The School and Society*. Chicago: University of Chicago Press, 1900.

Dolan, Jay. *The American Catholic Experience*. Garden City, N.Y.: Doubleday, 1985.

Dolan, Thomas C., O.P. *Theology and Education*. Dubuque, Iowa: Wm. C. Brown Company, 1952.

Dougherty, Jude. *Jacques Maritain: An Intellectual Profile*. Washington, D.C.: The Catholic University of America Press, 2003.

Dupuis, Adrian M., and Robin L. Gordon. *Philosophy of Education in Historical Perspective*. Second Edition. Lanham, Md.: University Press of America, 1997.

Eccles, Sir John, and Karl Popper. *The Self and Its Brain: An Argument for Interaction*. New York: Springer International, 1977.

Fagothey, Austin. *Right and Reason*. Seventh Edition. St. Louis: C. V. Mosby Company, 1981.

Fay, Jim, and David Funk. *Teaching with Love and Logic: Taking Control of the Classroom*. Golden, Colo.: Love and Logic Press, 1995.

Ferguson, Eva Dreikurs. *Motivation: A Biosocial and Cognitive Integration of Motivation and Emotion*. New York: Oxford University Press, 2000.

Fishman, Stephen M., and Lucille McCarthy. *John Dewey and the Challenge of Classroom Practice*. New York: Teachers College Press, 1998.

Fitzpatrick, Edward A. *LaSalle: Patron of All Teachers*. Milwaukee: Bruce Publishing, 1951.

———. *Philosophy of Education*. Milwaukee: Bruce Publishing Company, 1953.

Fuller, Edmund, editor. *The Christian Idea of Education*. New Haven, Conn.: Yale University Press, 1957.

Gallagher, Donald, and Idella Gallagher, editors. *The Education of Man: The Educational Philosophy of Jacques Maritain*. New York: Doubleday, 1962.

Gardner, Howard. *The Disciplined Mind*. Baltimore, Md.: Penguin Books, 2000.

———. *The Mind's New Science*. New York: Basic Books, 1985.

Geis, Robert. *Personal Existence after Death: Reductionist Circularities and the Evidence*. Peru, Ill.: Sherwood Sugden and Company, 1995.

Gilligan, Carol. *In a Different Voice: Psychological Theory and Women's Development*. Harvard University Press, 1982.

Gilson, Étienne. *The Philosophy of St. Thomas Aquinas*. New York: Dorset Press, 1929.

———. *Reason and Revelation in the Middle Ages*. New York: Charles Scribner's Sons, 1946.

———. *The Unity of Philosophical Experience*. New York: Charles Scribner's Sons, 1950.

Goleman, Daniel. *Emotional Intelligence: Why It Can Matter More Than IQ*. New York: Bantam Books, 1995.

Groome, Thomas H. *Educating for Life: A Spiritual Vision for Every Teacher and Parent*. Allen, Tex.: Thomas More Publishing, 1998.

Gross, Martin L. *The Conspiracy of Ignorance: The Failure of American Public Schools*. New York: HarperCollins, 1999.

Hancock, Curtis L. "An Assessment of the New Educational Reformers." In *From Twilight to Dawn: The Cultural Vision of Jacques Maritain.* Edited by Peter A. Redpath. Notre Dame, Ind.: Notre Dame University Press, 1990.

———. "Social Construct Theory: Relativism's Latest Fashion." In *The Failure of Modernism.* Edited by Brendan Sweetman. Washington, D.C.: The Catholic University of America Press, 1999.

———. "What Happened to the Catholic University." In *The Common Things: Essays on Thomism and Education.* Edited by Daniel McInerny. Washington, D.C.: The Catholic University of America Press, 1999.

Hancock, Curtis L., and Brendan Sweetman, editors. *Faith and the Life of the Intellect.* Washington, D.C.: The Catholic University of America Press, 2003.

———. *Truth and Religious Belief.* Armonk, N.Y.: M. E. Sharpe, 1998.

Healy, Jane M. *Endangered Minds: Why Our Children Don't Think.* New York: Simon & Schuster, 1990.

Hick, John. *Evil and the God of Love.* New York: Harper & Row, 1977.

Hirsch, E. D., Jr. *Cultural Literacy: What Every American Needs to Know.* New York: Houghton-Mifflin, 1987.

———. *The Schools We Need and Why We Don't Have Them.* New York: Random House, 1996.

Hutchins, Robert Maynard. *The Conflict in Education in a Democratic Society.* New York: Harper Brothers, 1953.

Jenkins, Philip. *The New Anti-Catholicism.* New York: Oxford University Press, 2003.

Johnston, Herbert. *A Philosophy of Education.* New York: McGraw-Hill, 1963.

Keene, Ellin Oliver, and Susan Zimmermann. *Mosaic of Thought: Teaching Comprehension in a Reader's Workshop.* Portsmouth, N.H.: Heineman, 1997.

Klubertanz, George P., S.J. *The Philosophy of Human Nature.* New York: Appleton-Century-Crofts, 1953.

Knight, George R. *Issues and Alternatives in Educational Philosophy.* Second Edition. Barrien Springs, Mich., 1982.

Kohlberg, Lawrence. *The Psychology of Moral Development.* Vols. 1–2. New York: Harper and Row, 1984.

Kohn, Alfie. *Punished by Rewards: The Trouble with Gold Stars, Incentive Plans, A's, Praise, and Other Bribes.* New York: Houghton-Mifflin, 1993.

Kreeft, Peter. *Socratic Logic.* South Bend, Ind.: St. Augustine's Press, 2004.

Land, Helen F., editor. *Holding Schools Accountable: Performance-Based Reform in Education.* Washington, D.C.: The Brookings Institution, 1996.

Marique, Pierre J. *The Philosophy of Christian Education*. New York: Prentice-Hall, 1939.

Maritain, Jacques. *Education at the Crossroads*. Yale University Press, 1943.

———. *True Humanism*. London: Geoffrey Bles, 1938.

Midgley, Mary. "Trying Out One's New Sword." In *Heart and Mind: Varieties of Moral Experience*. New York: St. Martin's Press, 1981.

Newman, John Henry (Cardinal). *The Idea of a University*. Reprint: Notre Dame, Ind.: Notre Dame University Press, 1982.

Nuzzi, Ronald. "Selected Church Documents: The Organization of Centralized Authority." In *Handbook of Research on Catholic Education*. Edited by Thomas C. Hunt, Ellis A. Joseph, and Ronald J. Nuzzi. Westport, Conn.: Greenwood Press, 2001.

Paris, David C. *Ideology and Educational Reform: Themes and Theories in Public Education*. Boulder, Colo.: Westview Press, 1995.

Porath, Jerome. "Not Just Religious Formation: The Academic Character of Catholic Schools." In *The Catholic Character of Catholic Schools*. Edited by James Youniss, John J. Convey, and Jeffrey A. McLellan. Notre Dame, Ind.: Notre Dame University Press, 2000.

Postman, Neil. *The End of Education: Redefining the Value of School*. New York: Alfred A. Knopf, 1995.

———. *Teaching as a Conserving Activity*. New York: Dell, 1979.

———. *Teaching as a Subversive Activity*. New York: Dell, 1969.

Ravitch, Diane. *Left Back: A Century of Battles over School Reform*. New York: Simon & Schuster, 2000.

Redden, John D., and Francis A. Ryan. *A Catholic Philosophy of Education*. Milwaukee: Bruce Publishing, 1956.

Redpath, Peter. *Cartesian Nightmare*. Amsterdam, The Netherlands: Editions Rodopi, 1996.

———. *How to Read a Difficult Book*. Seattle: Galahad Books, 2004.

———. *Masquerade of the Dream Walkers*. Amsterdam, The Netherlands: Editions Rodopi, 1998.

———. *Wisdom's Odyssey: From Philosophy to Transcendental Sophistry*. Amsterdam: The Netherlands: Editions Rodopi, 1997.

Reichmann, James B., S.J. *Philosophy of the Human Person*. Chicago: Loyola University Press, 1985.

Reitz, Donald J. *Moral Crisis in the Schools: What Parents and Teachers Need to Know*. Baltimore: Cathedral Foundation Press, 1998.

Rousseau, Jean-Jacques. "Discourse on the Arts and Sciences." Reprinted in: *Eighteenth-Century Philosophy*. Edited by Lewis White Beck. New York: The Free Press, 1966.

———. *Émile; or On Education*. Translated by Allan Bloom. New York: Basic Books, 1979.

Schall, James V., S.J. *A Student's Guide to Liberal Learning.* Wilmington, Del.: Intercollegiate Studies Institute, 1997.

Searle, John. "Minds, Brains, and Programs." In *The Behavioral and Brain Sciences* 3 (1980).

———. *Minds, Brains, and Science.* Harvard University Press, 1984.

Smith, Mortimer. *And Madly Teach: A Layman Looks at Public School Education.* Chicago: Regnery, 1949.

Smith, Vincent Edward. *The School Examined: An Essay on the Curriculum.* Milwaukee: Bruce Publishing Company, 1960.

Sowell, Thomas. *Inside American Education.* New York: The Free Press, 1993.

———. *The Vision of the Anointed.* New York: Basic Books, 1995.

Stout, Maureen. *The Feel-Good Curriculum: The Dumbing Down of America's Kids in the Name of Self-Esteem.* Cambridge, Mass.: Perseus, 2000.

Stravinskas, Peter M. J. *Constitutional Rights and Religious Prejudice: Catholic Education as the Battleground.* Milwaukee: Catholic League for Religious and Civil Rights, 1982.

———, and Patrick J. Reilly, editors. *Newman's Idea of a University: The American Response.* Mount Pocono, Pa.: Newman House Press, 2002.

Strobel, Lee. *The Case for a Creator.* Grand Rapids, Mich.: Zondervan, 2004.

Sweetman, Brendan, editor. *The Failure of Modernism.* Washington, D.C.: The Catholic University of America Press, 1999.

Veith, Gene Edward, Jr., and Andrew Kern. *Classical Education: Towards the Revival of American Schooling.* Washington, D.C.: Capital Research Center, 1997.

Walch, Timothy. *Parish School: American Catholic Parochial Education from Colonial Times to the Present.* New York: Crossroad Publishing, 1996.

Wong, Harry K., and Rosemary T. Wong. *The First Days of School.* Mountain View, Calif.: Harry K. Wong Publications, 1998.

Youniss, James, John J. Convey, and Jeffrey A. McLellan, editors. *The Catholic Character of Catholic Schools.* Notre Dame, Ind.: Notre Dame University Press, 2000.